"mimi tempestt writes like a third testament in which God (or our understanding) finally matures. Like a painter longed for by a million canvasses. No peer. No rival. Just a cosmos enjoyed by friends; alive in the most exciting mind of our generation."

—**TONGO EISEN-MARTIN**, AUTHOR OF *BLOOD ON THE FOG*

"*the delicacy of embracing spirals* is a ritual assemblage of flower-bearing armed spirits beautifully bleeding, brutally hewn self overstandings onto pages that can barely contain the divinity of the dance that tumbles forth between its pages. reading this book will make you better at loving yourself."

—**DR. AYODELE NZINGA**, FIRST POET LAUREATE OF OAKLAND, AUTHOR OF *SORROWLAND ORACLE*

Praise for mimi tempestt's *the monumental misrememberings*

"I love this book, and I think I won't be able to do it justice by speaking about it because it's experimental. . . . The book is a tool for understanding America from an intersection I do not exist at and how living, if unchecked, could contribute to the harms that meet people like Black fem folks, Black queer folks, and Black trans folks at those intersections. It's a book I'm drawn to practically, but also just aesthetically, because it is stunning."

—**HANIF ABDURRAQIB**, *NEW YORK MAGAZINE*

the delicacy of embracing spirals

the delicacy of embracing spirals

mimi tempestt

CITY LIGHTS | SAN FRANCISCO

Cover art by Brian Kwon
Cover art copyright © 2023 by Brian Kwon

Cover design by Jeff Mellin
Text design by Patrick Barber

Library of Congress Cataloging-in-Publication Data on file
Library of Congress Control Number: 2023938422

City Lights Books are published at the City Lights Bookstore,
261 Columbus Avenue, San Francisco, CA 94133

www.citylights.com

For Ruth
my mother, the first love of my life

"Liston's rule: even if you're acknowledged The Champ, the belt will be given grudgingly when they do not like or deeply misunderstand you and you will prance naked into oblivion minus critical acclaim and commercial endorsements"

Wanda Coleman

table of contents

ACT TWO

the wanderer's confession — 93

CODA

the thing about faith — 128

the delicacy of embracing spirals

ACT ONE

*seven **oracles in a séance playing russian roulette***
& my spirit doesn't feel like dying quietly today

i pray in tsunamis
riding moon-made waves
for the sake of this universe's inconsistency
parade around as drunken fool at center stage
                              & suspend everyone's imagination

the audacity for anyone to say they know me
must have the foresight to meet me before me

every day i wake up & watch my old renditions steal
my heart away from my mother's wildest dream
you keep asking me to tell my story
i'm too busy creating the world

basquiat's revenge

today...
i'm just a fat Black bitch with a few good words
a court jester at best
every [**Black**] poet waits in line for their 15 minutes
regurgitating the last one's sonnet into a lackluster spinoff

every Black man's poem reads:
i was killed today
i will be killed again tomorrow
america, you wish to consume or wear or fuck or frame my flesh
america, you were never america in the first place
let us swallow our fists until the bruising bears resemblance
of a broken chain
i am never at your mercy

they calculate every move
hovering to see if the academy gon' take the soul outta me
as if i didn't sell it already in a los angeles basement

//in exchange for a simple day

2016 got a few secrets on me

the devil got even more

i am imperfect
in the most perfect ways
no idealism penetrates the perilous nature of my pen
i see the southpaw stance of their spoken word　　　　from a mile
away

i prefer an unorthodox rendering of my wicked tongue

a fading table sketch of an early basquiat
turned calamity from a violent cadence

a sicko's mind fuck

how far left can i take god's third eye

let's see:

a portrait:

my latinx cousin smoking meth in the bathroom

in the room over her toddler watches a gay cartoon

a landscape:

my african friend begging for my hand in marriage

for citizenship in a country he's doesn't even want to die in

a still life:

of my third abortion. no. my fourth.

graffiti:

the line of coke i snorted the night before i moved to oakland

i play god always
i'm as shameless as i paint myself to be

the Black woman's poem reads:
i was raped today
i will be raped again tomorrow
america, you wish to consume & wear & fuck & frame my flesh
america, you were always america in the first place
let us swallow our blood until the bruising bears resemblance of a broken chain
i am always at your mercy

they calculate every move
hovering to see if the loneliness gon' take the poetry outta me
as if i didn't offer everything in a florida graveyard
                              //in exchange for a killer's aim

                    this the second time you read that stanza

              in the last piece

i refused to bleed
                    on this page

                              bleeding is the only thing

          that seems worthy of your applause

mimi, you screaming at the walls again

                              mimi, you shouldn't write it like that

     mimi, just shut up & do the work

                    mimi, play the game

mimi, slow & steady wins the fake   *mimi, tell us about your next—*

mimi, be nice

&

maybe your 15 minutes

will last longer

than the nigga ahead of you

the chip on my shoulder gotta death wish

the arrogance
can't even hide

itself

it removed my head
from the body
&
placed it off center

left on the canvas

---

the eyes dilate

lava hot

a whispering window

shot up from
skull
crack(ed) dances
into the yellowing
of the teeth
a cigarette spawns
the tall-tale sign
too good for this willowing scene
vibrating in opposition
to the onslaught reverberation
safety tantalizes for
luxury

i'm almost bourgeois   bored

the reality is if i don't hear the slit
of the wrist
transposed through
the paint
then what are we really dying for?

to be representational?
i forget to be here   all the time

GROUNDED JUST ISN'T MY THING

it's the ones who
prance proper
holy
who got the viciousness
begging   to   crawl
naked
completely out of their skin
me?

every wall

was already

taken

every seedling

of

doubt

was planted   into

a forest

decaying my wandering

thoughts

into a new beginning

let's see

how pretty

i can make

this frown

look today

casting call #1   *"Black (LA) woman"*

what the white folk rave
as the best poet out
of
LA

        is a Black magician's puppet
           fire dancing
           at the whisky à go-go
       on sunset

                little do they know
             he still ain't get it right
                 about me

"me" was
woman almost
on a decent los angeles day

               never cared too much
                 for the construct

      i cook up courage in cauldrons

considering against   the cast iron
on my grandmother's stove
    which slaved
sizzled the breast
of
chicken to cry
       unsatisfied in her husband's belly

at a young age
my hormonal capacity
took no stock
in the conditioning
of
her kitchen

on my 29th birthday, i confessed

the indignation

of

my conception

i didn't ask to be

here

my father giggled at the possibility
my mother stared blankly at her blessing

a loved mistake

i didn't ask to be placed in this body as time capsule

my mother's throat cleared   "too late"

to discover you are
a transcendental
accident manifested
through light speed
of
what the soul's been yearning   for   millennia

is the hardest throat slicing pill to swallow

my face blossomed   in a bitter womb
my two eyes   had to be inconsistent
to forget
the raw realities
          that come bellowing
                              out
                                        my
                                              mouth

my third one
got gouged
          out

          to satisfy
          a taste for flesh
          on the oppressor's tongue

             the oppressor's tongue got a sharpened fork for teeth
             the oppressor's tongue got a taste for melanated

                (i mean marinated)
                                        pussy
                the oppressor's tongue
             travels up my spine

                makes me arch
                  against the sensation
                    until my world is down
                    on all fours

i ain't got time
for the business
of
my lady-like tendencies

i am approximately woman

today

my ego decided: *i guess*

my ego desires
payment
in repetitive rejections
of
the pink bow
placed on my head   at birth

my ego said

    "this pussy is just an instrument you use
          to duplicate the nonsense
               of your father's makeshift manhood"

my ego knows
it never needed teeth
to make nice
with this universe's chaos

          my ego said "ask about me"

        "me" was
        Black always
        in

american
//invisible in a hollywood lens

the intersection makes

the contradiction

even

sweeter

my ego will two-step
& jiggy against
all their tap dancing pens

write about "me"

maybe

my ego's smile got c(r)opped
coon
on the front steps
of
the academy

i didn't ask to be here

my ego cried

"all this white man's theory gon' make a better nigger out of me"

fuck it.

i'll blame that too
on my inner child

in the confines
of
his bed
is where i][am   "made"

"woman"

he needed
all few
hundred pounds
of
my
flesh
bouncing on top
of
his small
frame

to   "make"
"him" cum

afterwards   he had a tendency
to reminisce about
his ex-girlfriend

this is where our inner children often played

she was sweet//midwestern

i am neither

he said he had
a thing
for LA women

me too

he said they don't
"make"
"them"
like "me"

anywhere else

this one ain't get it right about me either

my hair
       always burning
fire dancing
            against their fever
                            pitch
contend with
their tendencies
            to shape me   lady-like

    like lady   *i am approximately woman*

                        today

                i am

i war dance on faceless memories deciding against the rigorous threshold of a nuisance day. i spray paint my essence until the tables turn. music in back walls, alleyways of cigarette trails screaming tricks. what you know about a tuesday morning on a psychedelic trip down forever. where bravado is a fairytale of might could that never was & never was is the name of a Black girl gone missing again down sunset boulevard.

what you know about a LA woman?

jim morrison almost got it right about me. deep & wide into a quaalude of misfortunes, white boys with greedy hands & bloody noses whisper mind fucks into distant tidal wave of privilege as trajectory. in the basement is where i slaved on a microphone for five years. three of them i tapped dance for pennies. the two after that, my mouth found its way onto every promoter's manhood. i told everyone i caught a lucky streak. that phase is called the glitter guzzler.

where did she go!
is she here now?
has the poem been made?
where did she go?

what you wanna know about a LA woman?

she's devil-horned withstands radiant levels of torturing loneliness. hazes of hatred locks into infinite doldrums. begging for forgiveness for honest mistakes that are now too late to correct. i'd give you my tongue & swallow my fury if i thought it could save me. i'd close my eyes & never wake up if i remembered how he always romanticized the opportunity of tomorrow. he don't pick up my calls no more, he turned into a mexican mule. he turned me out & left me cold to call himself a hero. i'd drop everything i am now to have another moment just to kiss his jackass face. i was in love once & now once means never. his lies lasted as quick as it took me to get dressed again & hit the pavement searching for my next angry fix. i was just falling with my eyes stitched close. i was just swallowing to avoid a hollowing of time stamps disguised as meaning-making. my tulip memories have been reduced to loops of false youth. i was just running through that ghost city pretending to be diva. i was just trying to forget that my father never loved me. i was just fucking all the zombie men with thick dicks & false hopes to turn me shooting as star.

where did she go!
was she ever there?
has the poem been made?
where did she go?

that's when god found me on broadway. claimed i was an impossible thing. looked me up & down with the same contempt that holds steady in my father's eyes said, look at you this is the 10th time i caught you snorting cocaine on a sunday. late past midnight made a friend out of you

& up til dawn gotta a new girlfriend. you call it free-love-dancing, but the stuttering in your chest is a skip away from a full stop. so it goes another night in my 100 year battle with the devil disguised as god. & it feels heaven-like on this trip through hell. my body armor is a pound of sweat. my eyes dilate until my next target. a fast fix to the eternal levy that is leaking from my heart. this poem has been whispering unholy in my ear for three years. i conjured up the exoskeleton of my misplaced existence & counted three lives in a decade dedicated to the deterioration of an old soul. i am young in no one's heart. still to this day i would gouge out my eyes to be an approximation to my former self.

where did she go!
is she here now?
has the poem been made?
where did she go?

& all the theory in the world won't unwrite me & every mic in my hand isn't a confessional & every time i put lipstick to paint glory on my face, i disguise it as an opportunity to hide & maybe i was never reliable & maybe i was never here at all. & when they say she's a good girl, they are right about me & when they wish to frame me for all my sins, i hope they win too. & maybe i'm both first & third person & maybe i took it all too seriously & maybe i have nothing to prove but everything to lose & maybe my eyes had to be pretty to balance out the rape renditions that come fire-breathing out my mouth my mother has a more beautiful way of sighing through life & maybe i was always here but your eyes weren't trained to see me as i am so i became what i never could be & maybe this poem is just a terrible testimony & maybe a testimony is just a miracle come true & maybe i was just bored the entire time maybe i woke up on a saturday & didn't feel like trying too hard & maybe i've been trying hard my whole life maybe i be buying new hats for all my old faces

was the poem made?
was she ever there?
am i even exist?
is exist even an i?

can i redact the frame they place on me today? maybe i'm both first & third person, but always in last place maybe i was the big idea & when they say she's a good girl, they are right about me & when they wish to frame me for all my sins, i hope they win too & for all my sins they wish to frame, i hope i win too.

where did she go!
is she here now?
has the poem been made?
where did she go?

the actor

every audience tries to solve me like a rubik's cube

my true nature takes shape as a labyrinth

it's the ones who ain't spinned the block through hell

misunderstanding my full-figured salaciousness

calculated

they discard me

take on more measured women

clean

ones less feral

    less vocal   *more polite*

      their tongues

        like wilted flower petals

conditioned   *to say less*   *be less*

      poor tampered beasts

          unpronounced

& claimed   *my essence*

    a pity

        the very thing which
       draws them in

        now has them running
      out

my fangs

shown too soon

this time

when they try to retrieve what was lost

i could never be found

i'm too busy admiring my face in a handheld mirror

while sitting on the moon

the director

                    i want you to be demure

there is nothing demure about "me"

                    be a good good girl—

          show me the color of your bra underneath?

the star

he chose to forget
i am a deity
who swallows planets whole

he casually forgot
i require   worship
                 patience
                 care
                 pleasure
                 attention
                 adoration
                 respect

                his insecurities orbited me
                pompously willing himself
                into my gravitational pull
                he couldn't bear the intensity
                of my eyes he was unable
                to sustain from my pussy
                as our tongues connected
                i reached for his manhood
                a casual pleasure gesture
                a casual routine he wielded
                a casual   apprehension
                towards my provocation to
                expand turns out he wasn't
                so impressive
                after
                all
                when he finally reached inside
                his fingers burned clean off
                he left unable to admit i was
                      too hot to touch

"the poet"

on the cover of vogue

the costume:

louis vuitton kente cloth. rich green. presented as caftan. wraps the young

Black woman's body

draped to become more symbol than familiar

belt, gold plated

[from the personal collection of virgil abloh, himself]

a stoic, yet friendly, stare into the lens

warm & inviting

coincidental

proctored

the plot:

"representation"

"freedom"

"a stepping stone for change"

"translating critical race theory"

"invoking maya angelou"

the angle:

an inauguration of assimilation masquerading as riot

with every camera operating as gaze

golden youth smile radiates to be paraded as laureate

a doll of their standards

the poetry. ready-made.

blue Black venus

i. denial

at the gynecologist's office, she says

there is a poison circulating through my blood

says it's chasing the embryonic versions

of my existence like a minotaur in a labyrinth

i walk home below dirty rainbows

whirling in the dead-end of my womanhood

sleep for endless hours

dream in blue-shaded parables

every version of myself meets for the séance

argues over the provisions of my failures and successes

maiden mother crone

sits arrogantly against the reality of my fresh disposition

each pointing her finger at the other

unable to admit shame over my new set of consequences

ii. anger

he's to blame

the nigga who poisoned me

& the other one

who borrowed my innocence & traded it for a bump of cocaine

& the other one

who mirrored me as victim to our addictions

& the other one

who groped me at the afterhours

& the other one

who was too afraid to love me out loud

& the other one

who was looking for his mother in my pussy

& the other one

who deemed my body a treasure chest on pleasure island

& the last one

who refused to match my emotional depth

the nigga who needs to read this

isn't even apt to be on this page

my whole life

i've been talking to dirty walls

i'd smear my period blood

scribe *free* for fun

but dying was the only thing

i agreed upon when i came into

this cosmic plane

this revolving door of contradictions

this ongoing diatribe

of avoiding all the ways this life can violently end

i know i'm on my way out

i exited stage left before my first cue

act one

scene one

[*enter into an empty & noiseless stage*] from the wings, we hear prolonged sobs echoing into a chamber of infinity & doubt. MIMI, 29, a fat, Black & queer poet enters grimly on stage, plops her body at its center & locks into the fetal position.

MIMI

my life is now a monologue of deep **mourning**

i **will no longer** keep this rage locked inside my belly

& what happens when the **cage** is sick

of coveting **me** as catatonic?

& what happens when i get bold enough to stick

my head above the clouds & admit that a sunny day cost a dollar too many?

& what happens when i tell him **my womb** doesn't work?

i guess it will never be the object god designed me to be

Black/out.

the niggas who need to read this

branded me a "nigga-making machine"

they cry revolution

yet play cog in the utility belt

of men that gang bang Gaia

they parade around as moral men

*fathers to generations of goddesses downgraded to sex-slaves

*boys disguised as warriors who placate

their failed gender

with their miniscule dicks

*poets & artists brooding through their cities

held prisoner

to their transient thoughts

they plant polluted seeds populating thirsty minds

then laugh at the parable of consent

deem it a wayward idiom of the very thing

they claim they want they never had

man . . .

my pussy is metastasized into a doorway of consecutive non-believers

she finds truth in a psyche that's lost its grip

her name: none

her language: barely

the hour: wedged

the gag: their semen sliding into two day old panties

each droplet seeps into a stain of thorns and petals

bushed at the opening of her now pursed lips

the moisture is fixed

mumbles only at the crossing of legs

only at the entrance of his name

ozymandias

conquering time with a fever snatching

grains of sands filtering upwards

inhaling storms

eddies of indecision

to give birth

bubbling

berating

in fantasies

friction in creating life

mothering to dictate if it is worth lived

avoiding duration

    avoiding living

        avoiding temptation

            avoiding—

    you thought climax would be the next word

      you think wet is a testimony

    you believe hard thinking did too little for the heart

        my pussy

she clamps down   permeates until sacred

she bites until bruised   sacrifices & then leaches off the excess

she writes letter to strangers   bleeds for the full moon every month

she venus fly traps men   who smile pearls in bright rooms

she kisses foreign men   in dark alleyways

she's determined to deepen my madness

       while making bastards

         out men's strongest soldiers

iii. bargaining

a message from the ancestors:

this is not your fault

but it is your responsibility to heal through

let the tears you cry sting like acid

instead i popped a tab on Califia's island

heard the sirens cry from the river banks

my friend

she heard them too

she was more eager than me

to dive into a divine death

i convinced her that drowning

was the event that was already taking place

convinced her that they weren't beckoning for her to join them

convinced her to hear their lullaby

as offering

as reconciliation

iv. depression

i escaped from los angeles with a skeleton in my suitcase

it crawled out of its confinement

pulled down my blouse

sucked greedily on my areolas

cried *unforgiven* before it slept

made a scene about being wrapped in dirty sheets

claimed i was harboring a desire to destroy father time

v. acceptance

at the grocery store
an elderly black woman

plum sweet

looked deep into the barrels of my eyes   said sadness is a towering fiend

said he makes claim in the hollowing of your stomach

feeds you bread crumbs   then testifies that you've been fed pie

she gave me her pen & paper

suggested i make a list of the very desire i was shopping for
suggested that the key to getting over oneself was to revel in the reality of
being misunderstood
she told me my tears weren't nothing new
she suggested i continue writing into an untapped possibility

if you're lucky enough
you can find us
conjuring through a full moon
deciding how to ruin a man

the cue:
1. catch an ounce of flesh
2. name it merriment on the brink of
   obsession
3. lay a sunflower for synastry
4. add 2 plucked wings from a crow
5. spin in circles until your head leans
   north, your stomach aimed south
6. make sweet love to any body, while you
   moan whisper the beloved's name

she's telling me a joke about a character
whose name is at the bottom of the playbill
if she's drunk enough she'll pull out the costume
& stay in character for the entire night

don't you remember how to forget to be a tundra of psychotic loops?
this isn't heaven, just a simulation of ecstasy ogling to be imprisoned

she's mad at me again & all i have is a rose bush of apologies
i'm only sincere in this moment
i know this is a fever beginning to wish for an end

east la summer nights
burning beneath her skin
they don't heat them up like her anymore
the type of woman who cuts the type of woman who cuts

lilith aiming her gun at the center of my forehead
her chaotic apparition was sent to me during a night sweat
she lured me into a absinthe haze & mauled my cheek

fight & call it play
spit & call it ease
slither your brujería into my cypher & call it ordained

she speaks my hatred so deliciously
afternoons spent rummaging through her breasts
i want her to hurt me so vividly again
build a blood temple in the shape of her belly

let's fuck until truce?
you thought i was afraid of your devil
my hand around your throat as i claimed your pussy
was a hint of all my faces you were craving to see
you tease me on how i shrink in front of men that i truly desire
i hold myself back until it's safe for my fangs to show
you & i both know:
deadlier monsters understand there is paradise under a woman's feet

to induce cord-cutting:

1. **dedicate offerings to your walls**

2. **scribble hieroglyphs with the tip of your breasts**

3. **makeshift a barbed wire for a tongue**

i'm unoriginal here
i'm philosophizing
about a woman trying
to break my heart

i'll let her do it too
i'll let her kill me
the way i like to kill
others

4. abstain from sex with the beloved
   indefinitely

                                                        i'll let her make a
                                                        man out of me
5. pray to your goddess, ask for sweet   *dance terraformed*
   release   *into a rhubarb*
                                                        emblem the clouds of
6. call on your ancestors, request that the   *her mind make up my*
   incision be swift   *essence as better*
                                                        shapes

7. return the beloved's remnants. if
   communication & contact has been cut off in   *misspell the inkling of*
   this realm, burn them at a crossroads. never   *her fantasies*
   return to that location again   *enthralled by her*
                                                        world i'll let her make
                                                        two more

8. heal. meditate. pray. protect. heal. heal. heal.

                                                        i'll ramble through
9. integrate your shadow, observe the lesson   *the labyrinth of her*
   learned. be honest about who you were & what   *emotions be a*
   you did. love yourself through the pain & loss   *star-studded woman*
   anyways   *for her*

10. forgive yourself. forgive the beloved. go forth.
                                                        i'll let her
             please let me let her
                        place her father in my arms
shoot him up in my veins
                                                ventriloquize his hollowness
        disseminate
                    when it becomes too frightening
                                            i have faith in dangerous women
i can point her out
                    but won't ever pin her down

the oscillation of her lifeblood

goes against the sequence of her nature

i love her enough

to let her pretend   with me

she deserves this reservation

a foreign future

i know i will never

be her final destination

we act as stand-ins

to the next love of our lives

a tortuous pleasure

a reminder to her in my final letter:

i have no judgments anchored towards you
this was well-played on both of our parts
this apology will run out by tomorrow
you will only strike lucky in this life with the truth
promise to shake me from your veins
i told you i was dangerous
i'm healing my heart through this storm
~~i'm more poetic than life itself~~
how small of you to only think of you
when you had me waiting in the wings all this time
how small of me to believe i could own you

poetry is wayward attack from the heart

at the gynecologist office, she says
there is a poison circulating through your blood
you felt it immediately
when he entered
the orgasm was opaque
but it was the first time you felt alive in over 3 months

you spent that time being
another woman on stage
your world & hers
blended so deliciously

the separation felt like hell

you used to snort lines between rehearsals to feel like yourself every now & again

this was part of the fix

she was an emotional poet
not as bold as you, but at least she was honest

you had the longest monologue   written by a great Black playwright
you knew your character   inside & out

you barely knew yourself
after the last performance
for 3 days you went wandering
through the hollywood hills in a hoopty
with strangers
when that leg of the tour was over
you looked for a more chaotic disaster   you were spiraling

you can't even remember all of his face
all that lingers is how he felt in-between your legs
he liked to look you in your eyes while you were coming
he said it was a luxury

you both knew he was lucky
that's the name you called him
before he exited stage left for the rest of your life
sometimes you remember
                    that your heart circulates his poison
                        in your body
                                        every day

the exhibitionist just likes to expose her scars
after akilah oliver

she said. to her sisters.
one day. i'm going to get married. in a red wedding dress.
the bridesmaids. will be pickled. in all white.
& as she walks down the aisle. her groom's eyes will melt.
lava.
at the sight of her.

the dress will announce: *i am a passionate woman.*
        with fire behind my breasts.
        for you.
        with comets. in my belly.
        for the children.
        i am prepared to raise.
        with a queen's spirit.
        to protect what we build.
        with undying devotion.
        i offer.
        all that i am.
        & all that.
        i will become.
            &
        i am ready.
        to receive.
        all that you are.
        & all that.
        you will become.
        unconditionally.

she said. the wedding guests. family. friends. kin. community. ancestors. gods. goddesses. angels. universe. spirit. time. will dance. feverishly. under the eclipsed moon. wine. meat. platters. all. in abundance. for one day. an intimate orchestrated celebration. of joyful souls. testifying. to the divine...

WE ARE HERE!   *WE ARE ALIVE!*

what she was supposed to say. from that vision. a quiet truth:
   love is an invisible companion who has yet to make itself known to me.

i'm not running away from you . . .

i got tired of fighting
in july my cosmology hopped off the train
my feet followed
at a crossroads of   the past   the present   my future
i hit a dead-end at a cemetery
                                                    rochester, new york

i journeyed through a field of absent bodies   coming & going apparitions
i have an unobserved tendency to walk through graveyards
a habit of practicing a soliloquy or two for a barren crowd
a need to find an audience of dead eyes who met their final destinations

                                                    i greeted every skeleton watching me
i found her burial site without a headstone
my great-grandmother Lizzy
another Black woman   almost   forgotten in life   by uncertified death

        how many grandma Lizzys does this cemetery have?

the reaper who dwells in my third eye whispered *too many for purgatory to count,
dear child.* by where she lay. a willow tree. it was too old to tell tales. the withering
leaves knew a few sonnets about the grandiosity of a now migrated youth. under
a branch. a vulture feasted on a squirrel. the cycle of life made itself apparent
over & over to me. as i hovered to greet my molecular history. Oya sat stoically at
the cemetery's center. whisking the energies to move along in our cosmic dance.
i said a few words of grief & gratitude. i received my grandmother's apology. her
relief. she was here. as i am here now.

i return to myself

remembering that an unmarked grave gives utterance to the weight of my name

moon conjunct saturn

it's only noon, i'm six cigarettes in
blowing smoke into a philosophical time-warp

watching the dismay of an apparition disguised as a child
toddle over not being loved too good

the candid simulation fades into hell-fire of gods clashing
somewhere in my mind's valley these gods have a little bit of honesty left

integrity cries only for the apparition of the child
breast-breath youth mourning for peace & adoration

calming memories belong to the apparitions who learned
to protect their hearts before they close their eyes to sleep

counting to be more sheep-like than counting sheep
severing an umbilical cord make-shifted into a thorned-noose

swaying from the tree of life
thieves rummaging under a yellow skirt looking for a girlhood

the only prized possession in this crown
belongs to a soul's crooked crusader

all of the world's power derives from a clit
how you play man depends on the anniversary of your dying wish

ain't too much to fantasize about when the lower & upper half
of your body already conquered every man's consciousness

confessional affairs bruise a war-torn vendetta
the apparition fumbled about on its own conjuring

                  another twenty past noon, my eighth cigarette is already lit

the delicacy of embracing spirals

duplicates

a foreign tendency   to graft a landscape

    it dizzies itself to become
             peer pressured
                grows through movement as time

    the foot following the other
        makes steps sound like wind howling

all "i" ever have   *be*   the roundabout draining
        through the concept of a mind

    a brain bears logic
        when magic decides
            to leave the room

                i'm barely in my body
                i forget to conjure a here

i hone frequencies
out of possibilities
masquerading as sundays
           | take up space
           | take up moons
    "i" | swallow ecstasies
           | grin big

  forget a face
        is   *what trains*
                 the world's eye
                 to fancy elegies

a meteor crash of a serious self
like how drunk & high & heartbroken
the streets gon' leave me every weekend

laugh at the minstrel's showcase of a conscious being

who you gon' be today?

the tenacity fingering fiction of the human condition

whose face you gon' sing today?

linger to bellow without teeth
align to a cosmic counseling

fly not to think
blend not to blur
the lines of irrefutable irony

the x-ray of a melancholic poet:

drug-addled drunken demon
dreary drowning desperate without cause

who you gon' be today?

greet them at the astral.
tellem it was all a lie.
tellem this form is a second.
tellem to dread the spiraling.
to enhance the spiraling.
to force the spiraling.
to manifest the spiraling.
to embrace the spiraling.
to distract the spiraling.
to ride the spiraling.
to stop the spiraling.

to obliviate into madness & laugh
at the fickle trickster who knows
when to disappear into it all.

i forgot to laugh during the descent

the (in) sane self

the same questions

take it all too seriously

the iridescent subject

the channelor & the menace & the griot

the society & the society barking back at itself

brisk a dozen talks only to kill the self

i was never here.

i am never here.

the here is never here.

the moment counts down to consent.

singularity in the electrodes of a heart monitor

charred teeth

charred soul

frozen nodes of fate awaiting

the weight of its own feather & heart

who you gon' be today?

AT THE CENTRE OF INFINITE, THE BODY PROCLAIMED A BLACK GIRL CHILD.
EACH PHASE OF PUBERTY PRONOUNCED A TESTIMONY OF HUMANITY. YET
THE AUDIENCE WASN'T SOLD ON THE PERFORMANCE. PERCHANCE, POWER
BE IN THE VOICE OF THE CHILD. A PISTOL TRIGGER WARNING: THE CHILD
WIELDS AN ENTITY OF FURY THROUGH GRITTED TEETH:

the "i" be . collapsing
a primordial judgment
to step foot on
porous ground

philosophical unto extortion
burning passion unto exploitation
violent for preservation

be	*the rage*	*don't perform it*
wear	|	*don't let it get stuck*
break	|	*don't fold it*
fiend	|	*don't fantasize*
surrender	|	*don't personalize*
drift	|	*don't escape*
stir	|	*don't let it build*
feminize	|	*don't father it*
transcend	|	*don't let it become you*

sculpt fallacies only to tell the truth

be human always but godless to your enemies
be an enemy & reveal your palms to none
appeal to none & let your greatness parade for the masses

"ALL THE FORCES TESTIFYING FOR ME TO SPIT ON LAPSE, FORGET THAT
MY GUMS HAVE BEEN NUMBED FOR A PAIR OF 8 WEEKS. I WITNESS MY
FOES ERODE TO BLOODLUST. EVERY TASTELESS & VARIANT ATTEMPT TO
HARM MY SPIRIT WILL MAKE A STAR OUT OF ME. I NEVER NEEDED NOR
WANTED AN 'IN' IN THE FIRST PLACE. NO MACHIAVELLIAN SET-UP CAN
HUMBLE THE GOD BEHIND MY TONGUE."

who you gon' be tomorrow?

reveal too much *say nothing at all*
fish for compliments in a sea of sharks
dress finely only to let the wolves rip you to shreds

prance in their clothing every sunday
become a dusted metaphor or two
pretend to be a writer
fancy yourself a rockstar
scoff at the ridiculousness of a principled poet
hear the spoken words slam yet barely speak at all
disappear into the key of (d)estroy flat

gaslight   the imagination
gaslight   your mama
gaslight   your friends
gaslight   the city
gaslight   the you that plays heyoka on stage
gaslight   the audience
gaslight   your sisters
gaslight   that one man without a soul {who claims to be your _____}
gaslight   the city again
gaslight   the stage
_____   pretend to have a name   {AGAIN}

gaslight   the audience again   again   again
          again   again
     again
                              again again   againagainagainagainagain
AGAIN AGAIN AGAIN   again again
                                             AGAIN   A_G_A_I_N
     again
                         AgAiN
                              a   g   a   i   n

A_____g___a_i_____n

                A_____GAIN

AgaiN   again   AGAIN

          again

aaggaaiinn   aaagggaaaiiinnn   again

     again   *again*

           again

 AGAINAGAINAGAIN   ***AGAIN***

          again

   again

aaaaaaagggggggggggggaaaaaaaiiiiinnnnnn

           agggggggggggggggggggggggaaaaaaaiiiin

           again

           again

           again

           again

again

     again   *again*

      again   *again*

    Again

            again

aggggainnn   again   **again**

again   **again**again*again*<u>again</u>again

             AGAIN

     {{{ {{{hide in the symbol of the nucleus}}} }}}

transcend the spiral

die fiercely to be born: _____{enter a ____ here}_____again

          in the margins of this third eye
          a monarch butterfly exercises
          the feeling of you to be blossomed
          out of chaos

     honor the softness that craves to emanate from you:
      i care enough to observe the spectacle of myself

          charred innocence
         lingers its eyes into slumber
        camouflage youth impertinent to maturation

fly north to eucalyptus
      forget the previous iteration of a soul's territory
        aim to testify upwards at the sky
        build this life as a temporary home
        chime exhales
        brew a prolonged death

cry for no more here   & what was   & what is
        & what migrates a heartbeat of endless topography
      the truest shape of me conquers into regeneration
there are no values
stationary in this grace
just an ounce of face
daring to smile
itself into oblivion

in order to heal
accept a close proximity
to annihilation:
your nearest deathbed is a mirror
it looks a lot like my eyes

depart from ego
design a framework
composed of lotus bloom
let your cynicism dissipate   *magic*

dear nobody,

fever stiffens to be sudden like the way lovers are dispelled. i disassociate from my body to be a general to my thoughts. these war-like mosaic tapestries know more about me than what you will experience. a ghost of a drag queen dying on the floor. blood rings risen. an apparition's performance of a performance. a holographic soul displayed in-real-time. if real time is what we actually have. i protect my uglier truths from my judgments. leave the omissions that are most obvious like table-meat fat. an omniscient perspective is for the fools who rush to play god. i am much bigger in comparison. driven by the crows sitting at my window. the pursuit of power is the first thought that comes to mind before we put on our faces. a brewing hurricane swallowing itself whole like a snake adventuring towards its own tail. help me select the ways i will win today. press play on my life & rewind through every standing ovation. help me christen this plastic joy as my daily reminder. pressure my essence. get me to pretend to be good. help me be reverent enough to this pen to become a master. it's comical. all the sadness that sits in me. the only difference between you & me is the colors of our straightjackets. i've yet to discover the ways this isolation will take pity on my heart. forecast a net of a thousand inclinations to scream the same poem. i refuse to die kindly over here. or beg for sanctity. i have no love for jesus. i reserve that obsession for myself. here. have these problems. i dare you to hold me. i dare you to love me the way i ask you to. i dare you to revere my world. let's get this wrong. i'm trying to find the fiercest frequency of my voice today. i study them as they aim for my throat again. adversity always comes wrapped in a smile. i'll fight every nigga in this mind. they think i'm shooting for glory. the only heart i'm trying to win over is my own. i sit in the front row & nosebleeds of my audience. if your ears possess the insight to see this clearly then sure you can be in on the joke too. i've been called to say this shit. they don't have the kill to say it themselves. stutter autonomy through a locked-jaw. have the bravery to stutter it again. over & over & over to an eager body of wasteland protégées trying to be somebody. nobody, i am nothing at all. during the all. all at once. peeling back the layers of skin to erase the concept of a lived-life. i find a mood so solid that it trembles at the mercy of a phoenix preparing for flight. the theology of me creates this scripture. a violent peace of a Black woman worshiping herself. the gull. the cunt. the reality blessed to fruition. i'll have it all & let them drown in the deceit of proximity. my assignment of purity gradually erodes. i'll raise hell. simply. if i can't have it my way.

sincerely,

"me"

rat race; the mickey mouse in me wants to eat your face

they beg me   to steady my spirit   when they can't take
                  hold of my reins
            i'm still   dancing for   myself
riding angles   until the soul   can't break no more
passive weekends   with angels   sounding their horns at my bedside
blood gut   deliveries   received as pastel crucifixions
                  lucid revelries
                  brain dead on tuesdays
tugging at the wheel   like we gon' run
                        outta time
running through   the wheel   like all we have
            is time
                  grave dig into my ovaries
find a muted universe   name it lilac   turn it red
wishes writing   their visions   into a favorite
                  conquest
            tell 'em all   to makeshift their own
                  dreams
            make it desperate   &   begging for mercy
my lineage   never taught   me
            how to be
            just how to serve
                        i never wanted these prayer hands
i opted to be a project of eloquent violence
                  god is as real   as she never   was
            they all got   kingdoms   hissing
behind their eyes   yet fail to admit   in order   for
            a Black woman to worship herself
            as god   god must change

do you see the sky bending over backwards anytime soon?

why wear a crown   when you can make   claim to your own head?
             what good is truth
                     when all you can do is think about it?

decapitation is the friendliest reminder of our yearnings through
                revolutionary contaminations

{there is no way of all-seeing without being seen}

this is organized in every direction

i endow myself   as the monument   of my own fantasies
                believe in this life as artifice
        with ancestors   roaring   in the cyclone
                of my middle name
                        &
        Sekhmet firing from the back of my throat
                        &
        every item delivering as my decency shedding itself
                through my descent into purgatory

            the pros & cons of my faithfulness
                            renders me the greatest saturday
                                    sightings of me as a sage
less margery kempe more Roxanne Shanté
spitting cayenne takes between loads of laundry
with mama's expectations hounding at my backside
        the frenetic consciousness   of my body   holds more weight
                than the tedious posture of the poet
chin up   *eyes down*
            snarling niceties in the grace of fairness
            hit the mic & gravitate into a flow
            only to ask my mind's mirror:

are there passions that you have or passions that have you?
how many interpretations can be had before the utterance of a single word?
will you fall prey to the exhilaration & perils of Being too loudly?
will you let this paranoia stick to your lungs?
is this an antebellum decadence
or
do you have a blood thirst to go round for round?

my readiness is already being
{interpreted}   {hinted}
i'm always auditioning to be   something else
tell on me
you got it all figured out
i'm a tyrant to this fashion   carry in my essence
an audacity against decor
Black   &   unexcellent
human to a fault
a hybrid corpse   defying continuum   to become america's
most   brilliant   psycho
a stream   of consciousness   sold down river
everything   is   available   to   pollute

i been turned on
i been metaverse

being born   with only a touch   of reality
i refuse to be minimized
y'all not gon' do me how you did Wanda

i've   become   righteously   indignant   &   hyper   aware
of the whiteness   that powder kegs   this excuse   of an interrogation

my new poem: full of my ego
instead of myself

my los angeles melancholia will wears its hat again

a compound fraction

in the study of

undeniable madness

i've been trying

to destroy

this reality

since i first opened   my eyes

surveying all the peace   i can   disturb

if i have   yet to find my own

this is my new high

truth or dare?

i'll be first

i dare you to pick up a pen & not bubble-in a poem

i dare you not to sleep on any prodigious Black woman's soliloquy

i dare you to hold these words & find yourself implicated in the violent acts

that serve as the backdrop to the blood spilled onto these pages

i dare you to hold your applause to pull the machete out of your neck

i dare you

i dare you

around 8:46 every morning, i sit on my porch & smoke cigarettes while waiting for my classes to begin. this thing that i think i do. these words. this act of poeming has always been the rejection of the policing of my mind. i am an academic contradiction. an institutional con artist. i inhale the theoretical frameworks of dead white imaginings & exhale a brewing of poetic oppositions. i read the theories, claim understanding, then out of my mouth comes a boiling of puke. a hot pink hubris. a few blocks away on telegraph avenue, i hear the symphonies of police cars beginning their blood-day rituals. i know under the bridge of the 580 freeway is an encampment of angry already-ghosts. hungry mouths & wayward souls boxed into a frenzy of survival dealings. every second is a matter of life vs. death. i renegade against these melancholic scenes & find a fake solitude in my mind by feeding it falsities & convoluted fantasies of untouched possibilities. convince myself that the page & pen is my only hope towards survival & sanity.

for the 3rd time this week, i tell my white roommate that there are 3 types of Black poets:

1. The Love Poet
2. The Life Poet
3. The Death Poet

she giggles at my insanity as i wonder how all three types escaped me. i check my computer & another rejection letter sits in my email's inbox. it reads:

Dear Mimi,

   We regret to inform you that your poem was not selected for our upcoming issue. Although we found your work very compelling, the language used to depict your dead uncle, a Vietnam war veteran[1], was jarring and did not fit the theme that we hoped would inspire our readers. Quite simply, this isn't the blackness we were intending for. This isn't what we meant when we stated we were looking for BIPOC / Queer / Disabled / Activist / Inner-city / Southern / Ancestral / Diasporic / Chattel Slave / Fractured / Identity/ Porn. We meant to show us your roots plainly. Expose the complexities of the Black complex, traditionally, and uncover all the ways in which your identity can be magnified under a microscopic lens for us to harken on, and subsequently *celebrate*. To be quite frank, poems about the military-industrial complex aren't *in* right now.

Sincerely,
The White Editors of White Blasé Blah Review

my monday mornings are now reserved for whispering bullshits & copyright under my breath. i pretend to wish these writings were primed for proper positioning & polished poetics. i dodge the page & instead of writing a poem, i buy a frame. i declare i will adorn it with a sacred fury & hang it from a tree. at night i dream i am the frame & the frame is a runaway idiom that supplements its lack of understanding into a holding cell of bleak precautions as the frame hangs form from the tree its suspended self is rocked slightly by the wind maybe twirling about from the rope occasionally side to side but due to its tethering to the tree never floats to the sky or drops to the ground the frame me the tree the sky the ground are all fantastical elements of alchemy but no substance is ever made

i wake up.

the next morning,
my white roommate smiles while squeezing oranges into orange juice.
i puff away outside.
i remember that i discovered the fourth type of poet in my dream.

the first line of my new poem reads:

---

1 *the apostle, peter* is a poetic eulogy for my dead uncle. at the top of the poem, i call him a "motherfucker" and "the best story-telling son-of-a-bitch" in the world. quite frankly, it's a phenomenal piece.

Dear White Editors of White Blasé Blah Review,

"motherfucker" is a word that i frequently occupy.
~~*this poem got a motherfucker thinking that thinking has been occupied by white for too long~~
~~*for too long a motherfucker has been occupied by white~~
~~*a white motherfucker has occupied this poem~~
~~*white thinking has been a motherfucker~~
~~*white thinking got a motherfucker occupied~~
~~*a motherfucker thinking white has been occupied for too long~~

You see, I've never been interested in the formalities of language and story-telling. What is the word? What can the word do? How can it stitch itself? Stretch itself? Hide itself? Dream itself? Reveal itself? "Motherfucker" is the word I whisper under my breath when the river of life has switched directions, unbeknownst to me. "Motherfucker" is that son-of-a-bitch who owes me a hunnid dollars, and dodged me when he saw me coming up the street. "Motherfucker," accompanied with a *tsk*, is what i whisper under my breath while driving, as oakland pd comes (as they frequently do) hunting behind me. "Motherfucker" is also the enslaved son forced to breed with his mother in order to birth property, and increase profits for the chattel slave master. But you didn't want me to write it like that, did you? You wanted me to poetically placate my traumas and histories on this page, so you could check off a box to meet a quota of *equitable representation*, *inclusion*, and *diversity* for your publication. You want me to write an incisive, captivating, stark description of that one time a LAPD cop pulled me over on Broadway, and because he didn't like my nonchalant approach to his presence, tried to violently yank me out of my car. What an interesting (publishable) motif to reinforce the importance of *Black Lives Matter*. The movement you recently, and so publicly, donated a small portion of your earnings to. You want me to write about the pair of ~~white supremists~~[2] who attacked me and a fellow Black artist, by threatening to burn our necks with cigarettes & causing bodily harm, during San Francisco Pride as an examination on how white gay culture fails in solidarity with its Black/Queer counterparts. You want me to detail my Mississippi ancestry. My indigenous

---

2 my best friend william says that folks get canceled for using this word publicly. i didn't know my humanity came with a subscription. i wish a motherfucker would.

South Dakota roots. Sensationalize my heritage. Fascinate my working-class family and Los Angeles upbringing. So your readers can ~~salivate~~ celebrate the complexities of black realities.

*One published Black poet slams his repudiation of *this* police state. Out of passion for his people, he tweets (daily) we ought to imagine a new reality.
*The other one stopped sending in work. Says her poems about sexual violence and survival amongst Black femmes within academic institutions aren't being picked up by your publication or others akin to yours. She believes the lack of a student body at the universities, due to COVID-19, has created a disinterest in uncovering these former/current realities.
*The other one successfully publishes a sonnet composed of drowned Black babies.
*And I, instead of immersing myself in the dwellings and framing of my body, that exhausting task—that masturbation of painful memory-reality, make an incision on you.

The Fourth Type of Poet is a MotherFucker[3]
—she is the remarkable, yet very unpleasant,
thing that tsks while you gander at her flesh.
—she is the remarkable, yet very unpleasant,
thing who refuses to bleed on this page.[4]
—she is the remarkable, yet very unpleasant, thing.[5]

the words: the frame: the poet: the flesh: the thing:

refuses to bleed on this page.   *i'll do anything, anything you tell me to, man*
refuses to bleed on this page.   *i'm not trying to win*
refuses to bleed on this page.   *god, i'm claustrophobic*
refuses to bleed on this page.[6]   *this is cold-blooded, man*

Sincerely (~~go fuck yourself~~),

Mimi Tempestt

---

3 a justifiable hiding place.
4 all my life, i breathe while pushing daisies.
5 unframeable. bizarre. uncharacteristically abject.
6 for at least 8 minutes & 46 seconds, you too should push daisies.

untitled #4 (on why the Black artist is never seen smiling)

to those unborn who will dare to pick up the pen

when you open your history books. look back on this year.
ask where all our teeth went
our answer is simple.

it's not because love wasn't caressed into the seams in this current
    nightmare-life silhouette
it's not because we failed to wake up every morning without you on our minds
it's not because we lived hell in a year & a year exposed 400 years of a failed
    human experiment
it's not because we didn't stitch every word to fulfill your prophecy
it's not because every word stitched prior didn't help us walk in our own
it's not because you weren't envisioned to inherit the heaven that is already
    ordained within you

our answer is simple.
it's because our teeth were never here to begin with
every utterance of this poem is a prayer in your name
every prayer in your name is a possibility to fulfill a future
that always existed through the alchemy of our designated tongues

our prayer is simple   may there be less dead leaves withering during your fall
                       may your mind & body know rest
                       may wisdom reverberate from your lungs like air
                       may the words sing in your ears like honey
                       may you create & fulfill your own glory
                       may the streets you walk be clear & fully paved
                       may you make love and know it as the world's only gold
                       may each stanza bare themselves naked to you
                       may the chatter of their false ideations be heard as a lull
                       may you try & fail & try again to succeed
                       may you succeed only on your own terms

may your pen write in the same cadence of your heart
may mother be behind your tongue always
may your heart feel with no bounds
may the universe announce itself in your presence
may joy always whisper jewels from over your shoulder
may death be kinder to you than she was to us
may your life experience no limits or frames or cages
may your lessons be learned, hard & fast
may you forgive our mistakes & misunderstandings
may you pass your inheritance to the next generation
may time be your companion, not your cosmic overseer

& may every Black body
not be a dead man's
sonnet

& may every tear shed
on a Black mother's cheek
not be understood only
as a soliloquy

& may the laughter
of a Black child be heard
as grace in haiku

& when your words
find refuge on the blank page
write like the gods are
the only ones reading your soul

write as if you are revealing
yourself as a god too

our prayer is simple. & you, brilliant one, were always the answer

untitled #5
(futura free)

i. literary traditions as "the house" & witnessing the "problems of the house"
in the straightjacket of the academy
a conversation with a fellow Black & queer poet

my response in an email:

because i've always been a rough & tumble kind of artist
(the underground gave birth to me)

i've never felt like i had to contend with the preconceptions
& standards of american poetry

[i wonder how many of us are tired of tap dancing]

not that there isn't space & opportunity to honor those
who have come before us or even attempt to reinvent the wheel

for me though, there's always been an awareness of "the house," but the attitude
of the artists i came up with (shy & pretty Black punks, glamorous 3AM derelicts,
philosophical midnight divas spitting glitter & pure faggotry, dynasties of street
rats whistling ~~the avant-garde~~) was always "i create the wave, because i am the
wave"

we believed in our hearts, that if you play well enough & long enough
they won't be able to help themselves
> *eventually, they'll come & build the house around you*

& because we understood the house as fiction, it was always best to play outside
i'm daring to oscillate between two dead literary genres
a meditation in the realms of obscurity
they anticipate a performance
i anticipate whether the audience can can keep up

more fun & interesting things happen outside of the house

untitled #2
on the phone with cousin adonis

adonis:

*naw naw naw, nigga! i ain't catch no damn covid. my lungs collapsed from smoking
too many cigarettes. the doctor say i need to stop smoking these damn newports.
i only had a few since i got out the hospital. but naw, fuck that covid shit, man.
how you doing? where's your mama? oh shit! she working? on a holiday? damn.
you know what though, your mama always been like that. working overtime &
shit. i could never do that shit, man. sitting in an office all day typing & talking to
people. naw that was never for me. where's your brother? ahhh, that nigga always
be in the streets & your sisters? tell them i said what's up & you? how you doing?
alright, alright. i heard you was getting your phd out there in santa rosa or some
shit. oh, santa cruz! yeah i know where that is. but you live out there now? oh
word! you live in oakland now? that's dope. you know that's where the panthers
started their shit way back in the day. that Black liberation movement & all that.
breakfast programs in the hood & shit. bro but seriously, we're very proud of you.
i was always able to read & write but that poetry shit is too out there for me, man.
niggas speaking in tongues & hieroglyphs & shit. i could never understand it.
even when i was in prison they had writing programs for the inmates but i never
participated in any of that because i felt like they could use my own words against
me. but for reals, we are very proud of you. you got to speak your mind against
these motherfuckers. you should write poems about these fucking cops who be
killing niggas for no reason. you saw how they did that nigga george! & these crazy
ass white women, they calling them karens now & we all know that nigga biden
ain't gon' do shit. he fucking crooked like the rest of them too. you gotta write
about that shit, man. i'm giving you free game right now. that's what's important
these days. yeah yeah but, imma buy your book though. i may not read that shit,
but imma cop it. you the only published writer in this family. poetry is like a
secret language. you gotta be in on it to understand it & i never really liked that*

shit. i need to know what a motherfucker is really actually saying. it never did anything for me, man. but keep writing though. someone is going to appreciate it one day. & let me know when you have one of them readings. i want to hear you spit. i be on the zooms sometimes.

in a reading with fellow poets,

the host asks "why do you create?"

the Black poet (a woman) answers:

i create because i am god.

the first response to the statement
is from an old white poet (a man)
who makes an anecdote about an ape

with a pen.

ain't nobody talking to you.

go where you don't belong
after linh dinh

i found myself

tongue tied while asking ~~the critic~~ how to become a giant

he mumbled a premeditated scripture on meditation

he couldn't conjure a feeling for a saint trapped in a tree

i glimpsed familiar faces in his kind of devil

little did he care to understand; i borrowed his silence as a commodity

his language landed on me; this new scene: a sentencing trying to break free

maybe he had nothing genuine to offer

i've never been entitled to much

this wasn't my first meeting at the crossroads & it won't be my last

i've hopped off of faster dying trains

i've got everything

i know

& nothing

to lose

what a motherfucker is really actually saying

a chess match towards immortality is the braiding of minds wallowing against the doldrums of seconds deciding how forever gon' act. we bark at tea leaves. roam parables like loops forging against the steadiness of chaos as time then lie about meanings as if absolute. i didn't ask to be a poet. the centuries prior failed to execute utopia & i was left with a jigsaw to fumble about while breathing. the tendencies of my dreams don't know a damn thing. i'm mad enough to muse over this tyranny through monologues. one day i'm going to get it right while fully understanding that it was never meant to get got at all.

sun in the 6th (the house of unforeseen enemies)

you were in my dream last night.
i hope you are well. you & all your friends *were sitting on a stage. you were quietly meditating in the corner & then you left. once you were gone, people began accusing you of having a gun, but i didn't see it.*

how do we end this current american political system?

the elevator pitch:

i've always had this vision of Black femmes playing american terrorists: the true & justified menaces to society. i see us rummaging into thousands of masonic temples filled with white men & slaughtering them all like pigs. it'll be an occult ritual. one of our finest. they'll make sure to keep this out of their history books. it'll be full moon type shit. friday the 13th type shit. rivers of blood pouring into the streets. close-ups of white women clutching their expensive pearls as they beg for mercy & cry for their sorry ass sons. fathers. brothers. husbands. we'll force castrated dicks down their throats to shut them the fuck up. parade blonde & blue-eyed heads on pikes. sing as bombs going off in every police station. every courthouse. every jail. every bank. every monument. every one of their false institutions & diluted symbols. no warning shots. just blasting through every fucking city in this country until everything is burned to the ground …

my fbi agent is for sure filing this last draft for their records on me lol

you have to get down. this isn't a third world country.

as my mother gave birth to me
she fought with the nurses
while squatting on top of the hospital bed
she did what was innate to her
until they forced her to lie on her back

push
push
push
push
push

for 36 hours i refused to make my grand entrance
they should have listened to the voice of her body
its initial calling—
abiding by the law of universal gravitation
i finally arrived with lungs ablaze
i haven't stopped swinging since

i've been an addict much longer than i've been myself

mama i always thought i was meant for a music man i really had the audacity to become one myself with a silk voice & jazz hands banana walkin to punk bands here to stay 'til the last dance this is the blues' last chance to groan obscene i gave a soliloquy to the angels of this city & received their borrowed praises tomorrow i won't remember their grey wrote a new song to make the same mistakes i bounce to the rhythms & ride every cadence this high born of boredom is the best east la could offer i like one night stands boys looking for their fathers inside my walls boys dressed like men to avoid the pitfalls of this city that leaves them behind cages or lulled into sleep biting the top half of a rationed dream & street art smeared blood stains crying "save us all" i hollered godspeed to the little nigga who woke up & decided that the reaper wasn't going to accompany him on his walk today i make wonders out of stones & echo parks i drink wine until the bottle is empty my tongue flickering at the satisfaction of the last drop i hollow out i go back & forth with filthy strangers to make them envy the vibrancy of my mind filled like rainbows & wind growing like grape vines i'm so 21st century & i live for the people i battle rap & runway walk to help pump my ego i take trips to warehouses & disco like it's a crime kissing girls in dark alleyways & learning the secret to sex that men cannot find i make inappropriate comments in public i adore the old people they know the secret to life i can't even fathom & i know every movie sequel i argued with friends in the bathroom over the last bump of cocaine spitting plato & derrida through philosophical coke rushes & then chastised the white man's prophecy them muthafuckas owe me money again we hugged it out while screaming that our dependency was sane & it was & it is at the time i can't remember all the times i try my best refuse to find a night that didn't end in dramatic solace i'd do it all again to replay the relationships that never would mend the love lost i could never solve it nostalgia is my worst enemy my biggest fault is remembering the good times & how bad they were the moments of sweet songs that whistled at alvarado house & city lights like stars that twinkle & shine my love for this fake is like the sign that watches down on the whole damn race for women & men whose faces fill a million flat screens my love for this city is as real as the actor memorizing their upcoming line for the next scene the expression on their faces sadness madness wrinkles on a widow's peaks the heyoka repeats the scene to repeat itself again mulholland drive is my favorite snake running through this town i'm running faster not to be late with my never-ending date with the devil that's the only nigga who fucks me right &&&& mama we are meant to use things to enjoy god i had another conversation with my shadow yesterday he said i'm without a plot i said i'm the grandest chaotic symphony his ass will ever experience & a work of art should be regarded into an end of itself mama he told me nigga you trippin mama imma get it right one day they'll see as soon as i figure out what's worth more price or dignity he says genius as a backhand for inexperience i like to believe i invent my own rules for understanding me this isn't arrogance mama i swear your purse wasn't here when i walked in mama i swear my mind is a chess piece mama the itch won't go away today mama i'm constantly the guest in their house mama i have no urgency to the truth mama i'm hiding the interpreter again mama your assumption is that being in the audience of my disaster allows your mask to drop i'm a ghetto caricature of sunset boulevard this is the function of stereotypes i have no culture all i have is vision this is a consistency towards godhood diving head first to the me i pretend to be i was standing on top of the mountains eons ago i just be waiting for the preachers to catch up i guess i got tired of walking through these streets with empty pockets i'm not tap dancing for the sake of this art form the only heart i'm trying win over is my own there's a pot full of untamed women brewing in my blood i was cooked as their perfect ingredient to raise chaos in the lull abiding to this version of patriarchy watch me run circles around every man's universe the itch won't go away today mama yesterday's price is not today's price mama i'm not going to die today mama i know i'm Black mama Black as in watch all the ways i can die today mama how dare you tell a nigga she can't fly today mama i don't have to forgive you mama i'm not new anymore mama i've made mistakes & i have the scars on my body as proof they show me all the faces of my pain daring me to become a prophet when won't struggle be my purpose anymore purple dreams ensue like pigs snorting at the witching hour somewhere someone is getting fingered the acid drips into to the amygdala eyes diverted only to the house beauties i caught his glance he wouldn't me let go i fucked him in the back seat of my car his cum was mixed with sweet heat & fertilizer i'm incubating his baby in the coldsweat of this winter waiting for the salt of my tears to allow it to sprout i don't want your sympathy mama i just want to feel everything my giant heart wouldn't allow itself to feel yesterday this isn't real mama i can barely behave for you mama the itch won't go away mama the itch is getting worse i know i was taught how to love myself mama loving is hard in a world who refuses to love me back the new song i wrote was about another girl that song wasn't about me mama i don't sing about me anymore mama i don't suck dicks for deals them muthafuckas owe me money this isn't a bloody nose i wanted him but i couldn't keep him he was my lifeline my new mission is to paint my face mama how excellent it is to conjure skeletons for the sake of singing my ecstasy is all windows peering through a minefield of power i croon amongst gods who destroy worlds for the sake of being heard there is no morality that creeps through my throat just an eagerness to dress for the stage & weep every player's last words i came into this world conditioned to lie best mama this heaven is going to kill me today there is no pity in these streets & even less empathy behind their white picket imaginations at least the streets have a spine to claim a code the new americans became the feds & the feds sat back & said take a look at this our job is done the hurricane called my mind fancies itself as undeniable this altered state is the only comfort i have to offer the hurricane called my mind decides how to empty itself the sidewalk sighed unfortunate when it found me with naked feet its sits on the axis of pleasure & desire but it whispered something about a fall from grace i spray painted a haiku on the corner of figueroa & 6th to remind my handlers they won't get the luxury of my sadness i'm a fistful of gunfire the mathematics of my addiction is playing tricks on me mama i was never too good with numbers i owe them muthafuckas money again mama i'm still a gravesite away from being sanctified mama just promise me the day i leave this place will be the day you know peace promise me that mama promise me to move on mama promise to forgive me mama promise promise me promise me mama promise me promise me mama promise me please please please

mia, the mountain
on my neck sits
       a spiked collar
in my mouth: a gag: ball: red: spit drips
     hand-cuffed
         at wrists
i'll let us sit in this mood
       switch
violin chain-gang
        breaks
sliced jokes
        into mid-air

           "niceties"
     in my city
i mourn legends who knew more
about life   who carry a switchblade
   or two   at night
i've moved on from piss-stained streets
     the lie sounds better in kaleidoscope
you can't teach a decent revelry of sheet music
        for an audience who buys books
to prance bourgeoisie
every saturday evening
you either have the will of god behind your pen
or you don't   genius boxing up heaven
      to let the peons penny
their iconography for the sake of hell
crying about   a day off   all i need is   ***the heart***

mimi, the tempestt

the peacock tattoo caressing both of my breasts

tells every eye landed on

me

i don't fuck around

all the blue & Black of my

past   holds a

gift

my   grit is earned

i forgot to smile at

the man   offering me

a hollywood

contract

he couldn't

tame the morning star

out of me

& when he goes looking for my

next face

i'll be two poems

deep

gripping the atmosphere

again

holding the white gaze

hostage   *he responded to my song*

like he has me

stuck in his head

said:

the heart

| integration |

he won't find

another one

s p ill   ing   *like*

s p i l l   *me*

i n g

s

& can't replicate the allure of my likeness

p   i

l

L   i   N g *on the page*

something to prove or everything to lose?

it's an overbearing sensation
what this isolation offers me
i've concocted this desperation as intellect
chose a path that winds up the mountain
& destroys itself behind me with every step forward

i've sought counsel from the giants
men who sharpen their knives in their mind's caves
they sung in war-torn parables
colossal-like rhetoric of battles won & battles lost
they mirrored my missteps in their own trek through the same vertical

they chuckled at my eagerness to learn
they told me time was the only ally on my side
they placed their cosmologies in my back pocket
they hid their battle scars in plain sight
they fused with the journey & became one with its lore

at the tip of my tongue there is a dagger dressed in venom
i remember not to swallow my own words
the most glorious blessings & deadliest curses were born in me
in my third month of silence my feet begged me to go back
my heart understood yearning for safety is a myth

i listen for the crows' banter & take solace in the conversations between owls
i've become a nightingale to my most sacred emotions
the trees greet me most respectfully & cheer me along
faith is an inhale away from the desire of my calling
i'm a sigh across an ocean of doubt

can you hear it? the humming is one & many with you
how you hone this gift will honor the ground you've already made
the path of faith & love reaps greater reward than the method of brute force
head east at the fork until you encounter the black dove
there you will greet the sibyl you've been traversing to become

intermission

this is the part of our conversation where you tell me you had to put the book down. it got too heavy. for the first time in your life, the world was on your shoulders. this is the part of our conversation when you realize you're in too deep. this is part of our conversation & there is no turning back. go ahead.
take a break.
this part has been on hold
my
entire
life.

this ain't about you.
this ain't about me.

ACT TWO

the wanderer's confession

"supporting" cast

the heart   you, ancient, she/her//free

heyoka   me, Black, 18+, gender//free

me   you, Black, 18+, gender//free

the love poet   me, Black, 18+, gender//free

the life poet   you, Black, 18+, gender//free

the death poet   me, Black, 18+, gender//free

the artist as saturn   you, Black, 18+, gender//free

THE LOVE POET
THE LIFE POET
THE DEATH POET

HEVOKA

ME

THE
ARTIST
AS
SATURN

*what we're allowed to see. the house lights are on & the players are already on stage. the sound of the audience electrifies the room with anticipation & chatter. audience members begin to seat themselves & observe as others settle into theirs. the stage is the shape of a heart. a circle. a spiral. although there aren't any barriers between each character, the only allusion to the heart's four chambers is a t-shape on the floor that crosses it vertically & horizontally. upstage left, sitting on a couch conversing are **the love poet, the life poet** & **the death poet**. there is a coffee table & a tea set that they use to pour themselves drinks. each poet has a smugness that reeks of knowingness. their knowingness doesn't come from a place of earned wisdom, while their air of calculated disdain is off-putting & unnecessary. downstage right sits **the artist as saturn**, who is staring at the audience intently. they're crossed-legged & hunched over. they are mostly stoic & unmoving. like a gargoyle. only when they light a cigarette, after rummaging in their pockets, do they appear to be alive. every now & then, their gaze lands on a specific person in the audience. the artist gets off by looking into certain audience members' eyes. they are flirting. playing with their food. some audience members are into it. some laugh uncomfortably & try to return the artist's gaze. some look away & hope to never be seen again. uneasiness permeates the room. as the audience members settle down. someone else is on stage. it's **me**, sitting in a straightjacket, downstage left. their head is lowered. they appear to be aware of the spectacle around them, but they are caught in their own world. their face is locked into a frown. it holds the past & the future simultaneously. behind **me** are two empty stools, one directly upstage & another exactly at the top center of the heart. the house lights simmer down. so does the chatter. the spotlight falls on the empty stool behind **me**. after a prolonged silence, **heyoka** is lowered, head first, from above: their right foot is tied by a rope. their hands are behind their back & their left foot is crossed behind the opposite leg. defying the laws of gravity, a crown emanates gold from their head. like a blazing sun that will live forever. **heyoka** stays suspended mid-air above their stool. everyone in the theatre, characters included, stops & stares. **heyoka** looks out. there is a serene, yet eerie, smile on their face.*

heyoka begins.

heyoka   y'all are wondering how i got here. how did any of us get here? i
was born feet first & too soon in the middle of a thunderstorm. my
people were driving from colorado to montana & in the middle of
south dakota i decided to make my grand entrance. i was a month
early. my mother said it was the happiest, most excruciating, pain
she ever experienced in her life. my father pulled over on the side
of the road & helped as my mother struggled to push. another man,
an indigenous gentleman, saw the hazards on their car & offered a
hand. my father said for the longest time i wouldn't come, but after
that native gentleman came, i popped right out. my father thought
it was the strangest shit, like i was waiting for the gentleman's
arrival to begin mine. my father thanked the man who helped our
family by naming me after his spirit & i've been known as heyoka
ever since.

oh, you mean how i got *here* . . . i don't fucking know. can't you see
the blood rushing to my head? i get tongue-tied sometimes while
being tied up in front of audiences. what the fuck did you expect?
[*they look around the stage*] these dumbass drawings on the floor
look like four levels of fucking purgatory. y'all watching my descent
to hell, but here's the fucking kicker . . . i'm the asshole who showed
up late to the party. you motherfuckers have been waiting on my
arrival, so what the fuck does that say about you? that guy in the
back . . . look at that piece of shit. he looks like he voted for trump
& his wife next to him looks like she can load up an ar-15 in under
60 seconds. i won't say too much about you, bro. if i get you angry
enough you might shoot up the entire fucking theatre. these are
jokes, okay! i'm an apparition! it wouldn't be the first time a Black
man was found dead hanging from a rope [*they play dead for a few
seconds*] & this lady in the front . . . looks like the fucking karen of
the century. the original karen ain't got shit on you, honey! you the

newest type of karen too. karens get updated faster than iphones. surveillance on all ends. you the best recruit the fbi had on niggas since cointelpro. i can tell you've been snitching on motherfuckers your whole life! [*they dial an invisible phone & put it to their ear*] *hello! police! there's a nigger ... hanging upside down from the ceiling ... and i'm SCARED! please ... help me!* what about you? [*points to a kid in the front*] you laughing at your aunties & uncles, but you look like the type of motherfucker that says nigger at every concert you go to & we all know that concert wasn't played by the fleet foxes. you probably know more biggie & tupac lyrics than me. shiiiiiiiit!

remember when white people used to want to be white people, white people?! i miss the old kinda white folks. the ones you could tell were white. because when you know they are white at least you can protect yourself accordingly. i scrolled on instagram the other day & landed on the profile of this fine ass sista. she had chocolate skin. beautiful kinky braided hair, body banging! oomph! just delicious! tasty! just beautiful. she was beautiful! as i kept scrolling down her page i noticed something seemed kind of ... odd. i'm scrolling & scrolling & scrolling & her skin complexion got lighter & lighter & lighter. her eye color got brighter & brighter & brighter. i noticed her lips were less plump. her hair was more silky & by the time i got to the very bottom [*their eyes grow large. they take an exaggerated pause*] BAM!!! & just like that janae jenkins was actually mary lou anne. i said GOOOODDDDDAAAAMMMMMNNNN! it ain't good enough for white people to want to kill us. naw, they gotta look like us now too! like some hannibal lecter cannibal type shit. just skinnin' niggas & wearing us as meat suits. prancing in front of the mirror & shit. [*they do a series of model-like poses*] to the little white nigga in the front, hannibal lecter is a serial killer from a movie in the 80s. the funniest part though ... if i had the chance, i'd still fuck her! [*they simulate fucking by thrusting their hips into mid-air & placing their hands on an imaginary ass]* yeah, yeah! take *this dick, shonda . . . i mean, britney! whoever the fuck you are today. yeah, yeah! with your big ol' fat Black white ass.* ahhh, fuck you! that shit is funny! fuck y'all! you would do that shit too! if you're a Black man in the audience, some of you might be sitting next to a knock-off Black bitch right now. look at that brother right there! he's thinking to himself right now *i knew there was something different about her pussy.* speaking of pussies . . .

my homeboy, devonte, had an abortion last month. i told him to stay away from them atlanta niggas. atlanta niggas be fucking everyone, don't they? all jokes aside, it was a long & grueling process. it took him three weeks to raise the money from gofundme. then he had to schedule unpaid time-off from work. that wasn't the worst part . . . he's from texas. he was forced to travel across state lines to legally get the procedure done. it was serious, man. devonte is a good guy. real humble person. works his job as an after-school coordinator. pays his taxes. goes to atlanta every other weekend to pop his pussy just like the rest of us & he wants to be a father one day, but it isn't in the cards for him yet. he said he isn't ready to settle down & that's fair. i visited him a few days ago & he was crying. he said this was his second abortion in life. the first was before he transitioned. he said he never thought he'd be in this situation again. i told him *don't cry, bro. men get pregnant all the time & sometimes they abort their babies too.* i think people should have children on their own timelines. he said *i know, i know, but what if i aborted the next barack obama.* now y'all, i had to hold my laughter in when he said that shit. i love devonte, but why does every Black person think their child can be the next president of the united states? like its cool if your child becomes a dentist. or a basketball coach. a youth pastor. not everybody can become the president of the united states. that's not how probability or politics works! but he was sad, y'all. i had to comfort him. i didn't want to laugh in his face & crush his dreams right away. i said *true, devonte. that is very true in some universe in a galaxy far far far far away, but what if you aborted a mass shooter? if you look at it from that perspective, you've done us all a favor & we thank you for your sacrifice.* he said *fuck you, nigga, my baby wouldn't be white!* he had a point there. devonte kicked me out of his house after that. he hasn't picked up my phone calls ever since. so much for being a good friend.

yeah man, all this white folks wanting to be Black people & Black folks wanting to survive got me thinking. i realized nobody is safe. no-Black-body is safe. safety is an illusion that we give ourselves in order to sleep at night. everyone can be any-body whenever they want. for a price of course. but no-body is ever safe. we so damn backwards as a society that niggas who are alive are dead & niggas who are dead are alive. we have more value being dead than alive. just look around you. how the fuck can a hologram of tupac cripwalk on stage with snoop dogg at coachella? beats the hell out of me. the first thing my cousin did when the protests started in 2020 was get t-shirts pressed with the face of george floyd. he figured he might as well capitalize off the shit like everybody else. the t-shirts read GEORGE FLOYD FOREVER. i still can't tell if that's better or worse than a t-shirt that reads WHITE LIVES MATTER. y'all know they finna kill that nigga kanye like how they killed that monkey in *nope*. on a stage. for a Black person, the quickest way to become immortal in america is to be known for dying a horrific death. murder. tragedy. spectacle. that shit sells. america is a death cult. we know this shit. well ... most of us do. the best thing about death though, is resurrection. we looooovvve to bring people back from the dead. we love that shit! have you ever thought about who you would bring back from the dead if you could bring motherfuckers back from the dead? okay, who are some folks you would bring back?

from different areas throughout the theatre, the audience begins to shout names of famous Black people who are now dead. **heyoka** *begins to rattle the names off.*

josephine baker! malcolm x. fannie lou hamer. that's a good one! prince! michael jackson! trayvon. kobe. james baldwin. dope! dope! i didn't know white people knew that many Black folks. okay ... you know who'd i would resurrect? now hear me out ... [*they take an extended pause*] jesus christ & emmett till. it can't be just me! you ever wonder what that shit would sound like? the things those two have in common? again ... to the young white nigga in the front, emmett till was about your age when he was accused ... you know what? fuck you! google that shit. this is the kind of shit that goes through my mind, folks. stay with me. picture it. just picture it:

EMMETT TILL and JESUS CHRIST walk into a bar. JESUS orders a glass of red wine. EMMETT orders the same. Both sip silently until the pool table nearby strikes its first break. JESUS finishes his drink and orders another. EMMETT seems troubled, like something has been weighing heavily on his mind.

                    EMMETT
    I don't know about this immortal gig, Jesus.
    It seems like every time I try to rest, america
    finds a way to conjure back my spirit.

                    JESUS
    You tellin' me? I've been doing this shit
    around the globe for two thousand and twenty-two
    years.

                    EMMETT
    Really, man. It's out of control.
    They got me on t-shirts, and coffee mugs.
    Magazine covers. Hell—I'm doing shows
    on HBO now!

JESUS

Ah, young'n, it comes with the territory.
When Hollywood is knocking, that's
when you know you made it. Your mother
would be proud. They'll never forget about y—

EMMETT

They got me in rap songs, documentaries,
newspaper articles, museums, and art
exhibits. Even on the internet, they turned on
the white bitch who lied about me whistling
at her.

JESUS

Yeah, I heard about that. The big homie
downstairs is handling that one!

EMMETT

The historians can't get past me, the painters
re-create different impressions of my fish-food
face. The musicians are the closest ones to
getting it right, and the poets ... them fucking poets!

JESUS

Aww, c'mon! Don't come for the poets, Emmett!

EMMETT

Naw naw! Fuck that! I swear every one of them
negroes who dares to pick up the pen, writes like
I'm the cage that lives stale in their minds.
Like my body parts are the only words that
make it to their pages. And every year, they change

my name too. One year, I'm Eric. The next year,
I'm Philando. The year after that, I'm Trayvon.
These days, I'm George. Most of the time,
I'm Tamir.

JESUS

You can't be mad at them, Emmett.
Niggas is still getting killed by the white man.
You are the first made famous of the slain in
america. After me, of course.

EMMETT

Nigga! It's all the same. All their poems.
Me, the same person with a new name and
face every time.

JESUS

You think you the only nigga with a
thousand faces? A thousand names?
A thousand lifetimes? A thousand deaths?
There are poems about me in languages that
are not even relevant to modern history.
I, too, don't even have my god-given face any more.

*the artist as saturn, who looks quite unimpressed with heyoka's act, stands
up from their seat & exits stage left. shortly after, from the wings, there is
a rummaging of objects & loud bangs. it is obvious the artist is looking for
something. this doesn't deter heyoka from their story or interrupt the focus of
the audience. they are under a spell in a haze-filled dream. in the midst of the
artist's off-stage symphony, heyoka continues as emmett & jesus.*

EMMETT

Jesus. Man ... I didn't mean it like that. I'm sorr—

JESUS

You must think you some special nigga, huh?
Your mama finds a way to immortalize you
in every Black poet's pen, for generations
to come, and you have the audacity to complain.

EMMETT

Alls I'm saying is I'm tired, man. I'm fuckin'
tired. This work is exhausting. To manifest
every day in the Black poet's imagination.
To die endlessly without rest. I feel tortured.
Used. Ventriloquized. Idolized.

JESUS

Crucified? Like america's sacrificial lamb?
Deified?

EMMETT

I'm a puppet with strings, Jesus!
A Frankenstein! Their only Black boy
wonder. Their Prometheus.

JESUS

My dear boy. My precious, precious son.
You and I both know that this is the nature
of the game. To flow ever-present in the river
of god.

EMMETT

I know. I know. But I never thought that
in life and death, my nemesis would forever
be TIME.

*the artist becomes louder off-stage. grunting, muttering, heaving & groaning. flying from the wings to the stage, props: a trojan helmet. a king's cape. a small wooden bench. a king t'challa black panther hero suit. books. a cane. tap dancing shoes. bags of cotton. masks. top hats. costumes. through all the noise, the audience remains glued to **heyoka**. **the poets** also look up at **heyoka**, as if mesmerized & taking notes. the only person who notices the antics of **the artist** is **me**, who lifts their head to observe the objects that have landed on stage. **heyoka** continues ...*

JESUS

But if TIME wasn't...how could they
remember?

EMMETT

But if TIME wasn't...how would they
ever know?

JESUS

Time is all we eve—

*before **heyoka** finishes their line, **the artist as saturn** enters back on stage with a sword & with the swiftness of a stealth warrior decapitates **heyoka**. there is a collective gasp from the audience. **the artist** heaves over the hanging body as the head rolls to the center of the stage. with their eyes still blinking, as if still attached to their body, **heyoka's** head is upright at the center & is still expressive; oscillating between faces of profound sadness & contagious joy. after an eternity, the face renders itself into a perfect smile. **the artist** cuts down the hanging body from the rope. blood flows everywhere. **the artist** situates the body at the center of the stage & places the head in its hands. **the artist as saturn** exits stage right. **heyoka** winks.*

heyoka   thank you.

*from center stage **the heart** enters. she's wearing a red wedding dress & her face is fully covered under a red veil. in her hands, a dozen red roses. she is a vision. like a runway model walking in a couture fashion show: wearing off-white? patrick kelly? dapper dan? no. balmain. she takes a seat on the chair at the top of the stage & becomes completely still. stone-like. a soon-to-be person vibrating in crimson. as she stares forward, the lights focus on **the poets**. **the love poet** reaches for the teapot on the table & begins to fill three cups.*

the love poet   if you have a dream where you are completely someone else. with a different face. a different name. even a different mind. which version of you is still true? the person you were in the dream or the person you are when you wake up?

the death poet   i don't think any version of anyone is true at all.

the love poet   oh, come on.

the death poet   i mean it. everything around us is a performance. our job is to remember not to play into the roles of our enemies.

the life poet   so dreams are extensions of the performances of our waking lives?

the death poet   i think dreams are the mind's way of processing & enacting who we need to be to survive, if we weren't forced to act according to our material conditions.

the love poet   [*more to themselves*] so that's how a marxist makes sense of their dreams?

the life poet	i had a dream once that i was meditating in a church. i lit a candle. i prayed for peace. i prayed for clarity. i prayed for folks to make it through the pandemic. afterwards, i walked out & shortly after, i heard screams. when i ran back inside to help the people, i found that the preacher was the one gunning people down. i don't think any of that had to do with me. or who i wish i could be. i think it was a message about the state of humanity.
the death poet	& through it all, you still pray for peace?
the life poet	every day.
the love poet	i had a dream once of a frog & a scorpion who stumbled upon each other at the banks of a river. the scorpion walked up to the frog & asked for help. he knew couldn't swim across & needed the frog to get from one side to the other. the frog refused, telling the scorpion it was in his nature to poison others with his tail. the scorpion responded that if he did so, he too would die going across the river. the frog pondered it for a bit & out of the kindness of his heart, agreed to carry the scorpion on his back. this is the part that was fucked up. halfway across the river, the frog felt a sting on his back leg. he immediately knew it was the scorpion. when he looked up, the scorpion says *i couldn't help myself, it's part of my nature.*
the death poet	are you sure that was your dream? it sounds like a regurgitation of an old African fable . . . basically, in your waking life you are either the frog or scorpion?
the life poet	probably both.
the love poet	i always believed i was the river.

the life poet [*to the death poet*] & you? what do you dream about?

the death poet i don't remember my dreams.

the life poet come on! everyone remembers at least one dream they've had before.

the death poet [*hesitantly*] i dreamt once that i was in the audience of a performance. watching gorgeous women. with pearls for teeth. golden goddesses descending down double staircases. they hailed from all over america: nebraska. texas. mississippi. hawaii. south dakota & there i was. right over there [*points to the audience*]. next thing you know i was on stage & everyone was clapping for me. as if i had won something amongst the grove of women. i was placed on a pedestal. for being beautiful. graceful. intelligent. educated. well-spoken. i was almost perfect. i was loved. i was celebrated. they placed a crown on my head & sash around my shoulders. confetti fell from the sky & i waved to the crowd.

the love poet that's it?

the death poet almost. i went from being on the stage to being in front of a man. he was some type of ~~critic~~. more like a mirror. he was generous at first & told me all kinds of shit. like *one day you're going to be big. you're the most gifted one i've met on my journey. i can see it now.* he was blowing smoke up my ass. i was an illusion. not a person, but a business transaction. a small moving piece. the moment i caught on to his bullshit, things changed.

the love poet oh shit! like a love bomb?

the death poet   not … exactly. the last thing he said before i walked away was *this is the part where you sell your soul.* a little ironic coming from ~~the critic~~, but i don't think it sat well with my spirit. the dream lapsed. i went into a deep spiral that wouldn't let me sit still or eat or even allow me to catch my breath. the next thing i saw was myself. standing on the ledge of the 29th floor of the world. right outside of my new york high-rise. eventually, the pain was too much. so i jumped.

the love poet   suicide of a pageant queen? that dream is definitely hard to believe …

the life poet   it's truer than you think.

the death poet   true in a sense that we're all forced to contend with our own shadows. in the dream, i forgot what fear was. it was more of a resurrection than anything. i say tell the truth, shame the devil.

the life poet   sure. the devil doesn't like to be mocked, but even he has his own account about how things go down. all the truth does is change masks. what did the truth look like from the 29th floor?

the death poet   honestly … like i had power over my own death. which is something not a lot of us get. like finally i could play god.

the love poet   [*they stand up & prance about like a fairy ballerina*] oh god. god. god. god. god. god. him. god. them. god. her. god. god. god. don't we ever get tired of talking about god? god. god. god. God!

the life poet   [*to the death poet*] do you think that's what we do? poets … play god?

109

the love poet	[*to themselves*] goooooooooodddddd! god. gawwwdddd. goddess. good god. are you there, god? its me. god! god??? hello. God!!!!!
the death poet	god, i hope not. i never wanted to play anything. all i ever needed was a pen & a page.
the love poet	we're not god. or the devil. we're assholes. wide open ones too. the sooner we understand that, the sooner we will actually create something worthwhile.
the life poet	says the scorpion.
the love poet	no. says the river. [*to the death poet*] & a stage or camera! right? do you have the right amount of worshippers . . . i mean followers? you need a platform? a microphone to amplify all those big words & big stories & big theories & big authentic ideas you got flowing out of your mind.
the death poet	not really. a friend of mine once told me to be careful of the stage you build, because one day you might find yourself standing on it.
the love poet	ohhhhh bullshit! i call bullshit. everyone has a shtick. not just for survival, but for relevancy. all you gotta do is hit the right notes. this one is going to write sonnets about food deserts & gentrification in the hood. no . . . no . . . police. police brutality. social justice. all the isms. the other one is going to write a series of eintous about Black liberation & the revolution that never/always comes. the other one is differently-abled or trans or nonbinary or whatever the fuck they're packaging their humanity into these days & breaks language to showcase the disembodiment of their embodiment. this one is obsessed with contemporary Black iconography & the limited media

we barely get to create. that one showcases their lyrical prowess with the bones of the dead. the other one tragically fails at writing about her deceased grandmother's life in a choreopoem. you know … healing … breathing … trauma … bodies … nature … ancestors. this one is half-white & tries to make peace with their southern great-great-grandaddy's slave-racist past. the other one questions the validity of the academy while participating in it. the rest of us … well, we sit around writing about l-o-v-e while planting daisies that will eventually get pushed during the apocalypse.

the life poet   [*offhand. inquisitively.*] what do white poets write about these days?

the love poet   who fucking knows!

the death poet   or cares …

the love poet   all i'm saying is fighting stages breed microphones for the preservation of a consumer's fix. no one openly talks about how or why every good poet's favorite poet went mad towards the end of their lives or how the price of admission gets tagged on all of us. every guest-list titan sketches for safety anyways. why not get caught for hopping fences or spray painting the walls or shitting on their front steps? [*pointing at the audience*] they're going to fuck, frame, wear & consume us anyways. if it's truly a performance, make it a performance of a performance. they keep asking us to tell our stories. let it be a goddamn spectacle.

the death poet   some of us want to keep a little bit of integrity & humanity to ourselves. & whoever creates the most noise isn't always relevant, sometimes they're just the loudest person in the room.

the life poet	do you think white poets ever arrive at thinking of themselves or their work as spectacles?
the death poet	no, because fundamentally they don't understand *our* meaning of performance …

*simultaneously, each poet turns their head & stares directly at the audience. it's a cold stare too. glaring. burning. mean. the discomfort is thick. the only sound that can be heard is from **heyoka**, whose head is still oscillating between sadness & madness. **heyoka** is giggling, muttering nonsensical sensical phrases to themselves in-between faces. the poets hold their stare for an eternity longer. **me** lifts their head to join in.*

heyoka	the silence … god, is that you?
the death poet	[*after the poets return to themselves*] sometimes i can't tell if we're story-tellers or clowns.
the life poet	probably both.
the love poet	we're assholes! we think we're writing & then at some point the world is writing us. if we didn't have our traumas to front on the page, what would the imagination do? [*to the death poet*] do you think you have a choice? to tell a story these days, step on a stage & not perform? whose face are you wearing when you put that pen down, huh? you so hellbent on dismissing how i choose to paint this shit, but you've yet to identify the arrogance that is yourself. the crooked that is yourself. the contradiction. the rigidity that is yourself. you're a third eye blind.
the death poet	alright. alright. chill. so which one of us is correct? whose dream or spectacle do we buy into? what is the truth or do we spend all of our time debating in circles?

the life poet   i don't think "correct" is the correct word. why can't we all tell the truth?

the death poet   because that's not satisfying enough.

the love poet   or fun ...

the life poet   so what do we do?

a dim red light is cast overhead on **me**. *they are now wrestling in the straightjacket; attempting to break free.* **the poets** *don't notice any of this & carry on with their conversation.*

the death poet   what if it all comes down to chance?

the life poet   like flipping a coin?

the love poet   there's more than two of us. fifty-fifty won't work.

the death poet   i have an idea, but the truth that gets chosen will cost the poet.

the death poet *reaches underneath the coffee table & grabs their bag. they pull out a smith & wesson revolver: model 60 & place it near a teacup. next, they begin digging through the smaller pockets of the bag.*

the love poet   you really are an asshole.

the life poet   why the hell do you have a gun on you?

the death poet   *everyone* has a gun on them. *this* is america.

the love poet   now what? we don't agree with you, so you kill the both of us?

the death poet   please! this is our chance.

the life poet   a chance for what?

the death poet   our chance to leave it up to chance.

the death poet finds a single bullet, loads it in the revolver & spins the cylinder. me becomes more frantic in their movement. one arm is almost free. the other is tied tightly behind their back. they use the end of the chair to help loosen the bonds of the straightjacket. **the death poet** *puts the bullet next to the revolver.*

the life poet   [*catching on*] russian roulette in america ... seems fitting.

the death poet   nothing is more accurate at this moment than chance. let chance tell us the truth about truth.

the love poet   it isn't that deep.

the death poet   that's not how you sounded a minute ago.

the love poet   that was different.

the death poet   it was a performance. whose face are you going to sing today? put what you believe on the line.

the life poet   they have a point.

the love poet   that was different!

the life poet   to live & die behind the beliefs of your life's work? why pick up the pen if our hearts are not in it? you don't have to be "correct," you just have to live or die by the shit you preach.

the death poet   if you believe what you believe & if you believe that what you believe is the truth then put yourself on the line.

*me stumbles to the floor near **heyoka's** head. their left arm is free. they reach for the back portion of the jacket & begin the process of freeing up the rest of their body.*

the love poet   alright, alright. you're right, i guess. but i'm not going first.

the death poet   you don't have to. i'll be the first asshole to dance with the devil. even the being who is destined to rule hell must defeat satan. i counted it. there are six chambers, one bullet.

the death poet grabs the revolver, opens the cylinder & spins it one more time. they close the cylinder, place the gun to their head & pull the trigger. click. no fire. me is still struggling to get free.

the death poet   who's next?

the love poet & the life poet stare at each other. life begins to reach for the gun, but love beats them to the grab. love is crying, but through their tears is a fierce determination behind their eyes. they place the gun to their head ... click. no fire. they look at life immediately after in fear. death's eyes grow wider with anticipation. the life poet grabs the gun, places it to their head ... click. no fire. they place it back near the teacups. the love poet lets out a sigh of relief.

the love poet   see ... we can all hold onto our truths.

the death poet   there's six chambers in the cylinder. we only pulled the trigger three times.

the love poet   we left it up to chance. those were our chances.

the death poet   i want to know the truth.

the love poet   why? you have something to prove?

the death poet	don't you want to know? how far you're willing to go for the sake of your truth? for the sake of your craft?
the love poet	i don't have a death wish. i'm just trying to get by.
the death poet	that! that's it! you said it. you'll put on whatever mask is necessary to tap dance on that damn stage! how do you not see that as a problem?
the love poet	i'll do anything to continue doing what i love most. sacrificing for what or who you love is inevitable sometimes.
the life poet	i don't agree. why not make it unique to you? do what's true to you. resist the expectation of the gaze. why does it always have to be a performance? if you love it so much. own it. make it yours. i want to know the truth too.
the love poet	i never thought i had a choi—

the life poet *grabs the revolver, places it to their head & pulls the trigger. fire!* ***life*** *is dead on the couch. their blood & brain is a feast sprawled everywhere.* ***love*** *lets out a shriek that radiates like an atomic bomb throughout the entire theatre.* ***death*** *looks stunned.* ***me*** *still struggles to break free on the floor.*

me	this is a nightmare!

the death poet *reaches for the revolver & the bullets.*

the love poet	no. no. no. no.no.no. it's over. we got our answer.
the death poet	[*loading the gun*] no. that's not it. we're both still here. that means one of us is wrong or right.

the love poet   please stop. please. i was in love with life. they never loved me back, but it didn't stop me from trying & sticking around. even if i made a fool of myself. i was always learning from life. why do you think i'm still here? please … no more.

the death poet loads the revolver & places it to their head. right before they pull the trigger, love lunges over to stop death. the revolver is knocked to the floor. me breaks free from their straightjacket. love & death wrestle on the couch on top of life's body. death gains an advantage & begins to strangle love. love turns blue. then purple. their eyes roll to the back of their head & eventually they pass out. me crawls past heyoka & grabs the gun. they stand on their feet & shoot the death poet at the back of their head. me pulls death's body off of the love poet & checks for a pulse. the love poet is dead too. me lets out a scream of rage & sadness. they place the gun to their head. click. no fire. click. no fire. click. no fire. click. no fire. click. no fire. click. no fire.

Black/out.

the piano keys of "suzanne" by nina simone call out in the dark. the stage becomes dimly lit & radiates different hues: reds, purples, blues, greens, yellows, oranges. **the heart** *stands up from her seat & begins to walk on the outer traces of the stage. clockwise. the walk is slow, but determined. she moves in accordance with the rhythm of the song, dropping roses from her bouquet as she goes.*

"suzanne takes you down to her place by the river"

me *is sitting limply amongst the dead poets. they drop the gun on the coffee table, stand up & walk grimly to center stage; plopping their body next to* **heyoka** *& lock into the fetal position.*

"and you know that she's half-crazy. that's why you want to be there"

heyoka *is crying. their expression is desperately sad. the mouth is elongated & turned into a perpetual frown. their face is exaggerated, as if they are wearing a mask of melpomene. the tears flow & flow & flow, creating a puddle beneath them. the hands of their body pat the head to console them.*

"and you want to travel with her. and you want to travel blind"

the heart *continues to travel in circles. with every complete cycle, she picks up speed.* **the artist as saturn** *enters from stage right. they are carrying an easel, a canvas, a bag with painting & graffiti supplies. they walk over to the dead poets & begin moving the bodies to make space to work.*

"you've touched her perfect body with your mind"

they place **the death poet** on the ground. **the love poet** & **the life poet** are seated on the couch in a lovers' embrace. **the artist as saturn** sets their easel & canvas in front of the empty seat. they grab the gun on the coffee table & reach into **death's** bag, searching for bullets.

"now jesus was a sailor. when he walked upon the water"

they load the gun, place it on the armrest of the couch. they swipe the table clean of all objects; three teacups, the teapot & **death's** bag. they place their own bag on top of the coffee table, light a cigarette & continue setting up their materials to begin painting. they start off with a pencil to sketch at first & then begin prepping their brushes & palette.

"but he himself was broken. long before the sky would open."

"forsaken. almost human"

the heart is pacing now. round & round & round she goes. **heyoka's** crying turns into uncontrollable sobs. **me** lies beside them. still. motionless. stunned. a ghost of the environment. **the artist as saturn** is at work on the canvas.

"and she shows you where to look between the garbage and the flowers"

the heart is running now. round & round & round she goes. you notice **the artist as saturn** is using the blood of **the poets** to fill their palette. they dip their brush in the blood & work on the canvas. occasionally they look up to observe the audience.

"there are heroes in the seaweed. there are children in the morning"

"they are leaning out for love and they will lean that way forever"

the stage lights continue to rain different hues: reds, purples, blues, greens, yellows, oranges. the change of colors is more frequent. frantic. **heyoka** is no longer crying. they are now laughing, excessively happy. the mouth is elongated & turned into a perpetual smile. their face is exaggerated, as if they are wearing a mask of thalia. the laughter rings & rings & rings creating an echo around them. the hands of their body lift the head to amplify the sound.

"while suzanne holds the mirror"

the heart is running. **heyoka** is laughing. **the artist as saturn** is painting. **me** stands on their feet & walks to the front of the stage. the stage lights are dancing: reds, purples, blues, greens, yellows, oranges. reds, purples, blues, greens, yellows, oranges. reds, purples, blues, greens, yellows, oranges. reds, purples, blues, greens, yellows, oranges.

"and you want to travel with her. and you want to travel blind"

"you think maybe you can trust her."

"she's touched your perfect body with her mind"

the songs ends. **the heart** returns slowly to her seat. **heyoka** holds a blank stare. **the artist as saturn** puts their brush down & lights another cigarette. the lights have ceased. a spotlight is now on **me**.

me   the truth is a precarious situation. the stage is four chambers of an injured heart (not completely broken) & in it lies a consciousness waiting to croon. the mind. the body. the stomach. even the feet know when to abstain from danger, but the heart understands none of this. its only function is to trudge on. the heart, like saturn, is the cosmic ruler of time. the heart, like venus, siezes every opportunity to create a target for eros to shoot. the heart, like jupiter, knows only to expand forth from nothing into light. none of this is new. to you. to me & because of this agreement, i offer you the enjoyment in the spectacle of me. knowing that it is me who is enacting the spectacle of you. a lick of shadows & mirrors. the scene is a precarious situation & it takes place everywhere. all the time. it's a funhouse attraction at the traveling carnival. it's two young lovers making a baby in the backseat of a car. it's oshun on the 98th brush stroke of her hair while waiting violently on the moon. it's matangi eating leftovers as offerings & accepting remnants with menses at the crossroads. it's a caravan crash of small children heading to school in colima. it's two African immigrant men cruising for each other in a supermarket in london. it's a protest by & for indigenous women to find their missing girls in montreal. it's 2034. it's shiva being stunned out of his meditation by kama to finally glimpse the beauty of parvati. it's a millennial tattoo artist from brazil following her calling to become a ghetto shaman. it's a hurricane devastating the coasts of bali. it's a dream of a 100-year war in the psyche of a jamaican man on his deathbed in kagoshima. it's the birth of a firstborn child to a puerto rican gay couple in new york. it's anansi stealing the world's wisdom from the sky god. it's fraternal twins, who hated each other all their lives, holding hands at the end of the world. it's a loving uncle in eagle rock slowing eroding through his dementia. it's a spiral.

the truth is a precarious situation & it's happening anywhere. everytime. it's a new bookstore owner in san francisco being guided by the love of his ancestors. it's a 23-year-old student in kolkata trying to come to america to get her phd. it's a brown woman in san antonio withered by time waiting for her lover to return home from prison. it's the date rape in the basement of an underground party in lagos. it's a young creole woman from fresno copying the style & mannerisms of other Black women to fake an authentic personality. it's 1969. it's an up & coming singer from chicago traveling to berlin in his final attempt to make it big. it's a working-class security guard trekking to paris to deliver a million-dollar necklace to a billionaire's wife. it's a 2nd grade teacher living with ptsd after her entire classroom of students was killed in a school shooting. it's tonantzín changing her name to the virgen de guadalupe. it's a chilean sculptor finally feeling seen by her father. it's brown babies in cages. it's a brother & sister from compton arguing with each other because they love each other the most. it's miss usa jumping off the 29th floor of her new york city high-rise apartment. it's an image of relations instead of a vision of the whole world. it's a vietnamese man using his alchemy to express his love for his community through home-cooked meals. it's the deep misunderstanding of words & intentions between two great, yet stubborn, poets. it's genuine vulnerability flowering out of one's heart after decades of wearing a stoic false mask. it's ganesha wailing his trunk at a poor toddler who is destined for greatness in this lifetime. it's a dirty & hilarious meme spread on the internet. it's the political prisoners rotting in cells wondering what death will be like in their next incarnations. it's kuan yin hearing a mother's cry & answering her prayers. it's a selfie with a popstar on stage at the festival in portimão. it's the psychological abuse of one righteous police officer amongst a dogpile of pigs. it's being sentenced to serve 9.5 years in a russian prison for having traces of weed in your carry-on. it's being in love with someone who doesn't have the emotional bandwidth to love you back. it's remembering the entire west coast of the u.s. can wake up on mars anyday. it's finally jumping over the broom with the love of your life. it's an adopted boy, now a woman, driving to tampa with her own daughter, ready to meet her birth mother for the first time. the truth is a precarious situation & it's happening & happening & happ—

*they lie back down & lock into the fetal position once again. **the heart** stands & makes her way from her seat directly to **me**; gently stepping over **heyoka's** head & body along the way. **the heart** lifts **me**, cradles them gently in her arms & walks off stage into the audience. they continue together, down the main aisle of the theatre & never look back.*

*the entire theatre is red now: it descended from the stage as **the heart** & **me** walked into eternity. it's an eerie red, reminiscent of human flesh. like the arteries & internal organs of the body are being exposed. **the artist as saturn** works diligently on the canvas between cigarettes. **heyoka's** body is petting its own head. for the first time, there is a genuine expression of peace across their face. **the artist as saturn** takes a step back from their work & studies it. without showing it to the audience, they carefully bring the easel & the painting to center stage. about a foot in front of **heyoka**. they walk to the couch, grab the revolver from the arm rest & return to the easel. they light another cigarette & turn the painting around for the eyes to see. the portrait is of the faces in the dark. from the first row. to the mezzanine. even those seated in the balcony. all magnified & exaggerated. the collection of faces as skulls as masks. the eyes protruding from the sockets. different impressions. lines of graffiti amongst brush strokes. teeth exposed. every single face. gasping. applauding. smiling. crying. shaking. hiding. the portrait is a mirror capturing every audience member in the theatre. **the artist as saturn** grabs **heyoka's** head & places it under their left armpit. they aim the revolver at the audience.*

the artist as saturn   you motherfuckers owe me. the bidding begins now. for my life/work, the price of this auction starts at $110.5 million. that's the minimum to see me sweat.

audience member #1 $111 million!

***the artist as saturn** shoots the woman in the fourth row who raised her hand.*

audience member #2 $120 million!

***the artist as saturn** shoots the gentlemen in the front who is waving his wallet.*

audience member #3 $195 million!

the artist as saturn shoots the person walking towards the stage holding a diamond necklace.

audience member #4 $200.6 million!

the artist as saturn shoots three more people in the audience. their eyes become wilder & more deranged after every shot. they were especially brazen for the woman in the front who tried to run towards safety. they walk back to the couch, place **heyoka's** head on the coffee table, & reload the revolver with more bullets.

audience member #5 $336 million!

voices from the audience $512 million!

$575.4 million!

$666 million!

the artist as saturn picks up **heyoka** again, returns to the painting while aiming at the audience & shoots & shoots & shoots & shoots & shoots & shoots. higher bids ring throughout the theatre. there's a chaotic symphony of millions being hurled at *the artist*. with every six shots, they reload the revolver again. repeating the task more vigorously each time. they eventually walk into the crowd. where you've been sitting this whole time. watching. spectating. lurking. their hovering is ominous. unescapable. they look at *you*. meet your gaze & place the gun right between your eyes. click. fire.

end

after taking a bow

with bloody roses in hand

the curtains close

applause

CODA

the thing about faith:

My father always tells me this story, and it's a story that I consider every time my life has hit a dead end or slowed down immensely. The eldest of my siblings are what you would call "Irish triplets," meaning that we were all born 11 months apart. Sheila, who is the youngest of the three, was born in less than 6 hours, and although she arrived with the umbilical cord wrapped around her neck, her arrival was mostly smooth. In some African traditions, being born with the umbilical cord around your neck is a sign of one being destined for great leadership. My father jokes that before he finished tying his shoes to head over to the hospital, she was already here. Shelton Jr., the middle child, was born in under 10 hours with mild complications. And although his birth was mostly easy, my father notes that my brother spent the first year of his life crying about his arrival. I, the oldest of the trio, took 36 hours of labor. After hours of struggling and arguments between my mother, my grandmother, the nurses, and the doctor, I finally arrived. Both my parents comment that I came onto this plane quiet, wide-eyed, and very observant of my environment. My father tells me this story periodically, because he believes our birth stories are correlated to how we experience success in our lives.

Sheila became a Basketball prodigy by the time she was 10 years old. She has known and still achieves huge leaps of success in her respected field. She's on her way to becoming a great coach, and comes from a Basketball lineage connected to the teachings of Pat Summit. Shelton, although having taken many paths with many twists and turns, is like a cat with 9 lives. He always lands on his feet. He's traveled the world playing professional Basketball, and returns with stories about each country's political and socio-economic landscape. He's worldwide and transformative. He is the king of rebirth; the only man I know who shook hands with Death, and came back with a story of a lifetime. He's free-spirited, wild-minded, and assured in his views of the world based on his experiences. He measures success and contentment by his own terms.

Life hasn't always been kind to me. I am not an athlete like my siblings. I am sensitive and artistic. Queer and intuitive. My life, up until four years ago, was like one large trek up a ridiculous mountain. I've endured my demons, fought them, created new ones, and then fought them again. I don't like the badges of "victim" or "survivor" for myself, but I can acknowledge that my journey has made me headstrong, cautious, and determined. I take none of my success and opportunities for granted. I will always be grateful for the small things. All my siblings and I come with our own set of unique strengths and weaknesses, but we all have the spirit of warriors. I framed the archetypes of the three poets on this parable made by my father. Choosing to honor our familial folklore.

My father, a sarcastic Leo moon, believes my arrival to my fullest potential and success won't come until much later in my life. He is proven to be prophetic in strange ways. He's a trickster and teaches his lessons through off-handed jokes, cheesy one-liners, and parables. I don't know whether to be thankful for his premonitions or to be bull-headed in the creation of my destiny. I know he tells me this story to remind me to honor the resilience needed for my path and to celebrate how far I've come. It's his special way of saying *I love you, and I see how hard you work.* He always ends this story with "Mia, your path doesn't look like anybody else's. For our family, your trajectory is less traveled. Your time in the sun will come. And when it does ... nobody can tell you shit, because you wanted it and you earned it!" I wrote this book wondering: *What is the performance of my story? Do I want to tell the truth? What the fuck is truth anyways? Isn't this shit all a farce? How can I tell you where I begin and end, if I haven't even arrived?* This book is a pit stop. A small breather. An observation of the map before I move to the next leg of my trip. I needed a water break.

Thank you for joining me on the journey, so far. I didn't take myself as a subject too seriously, and if you somehow witnessed yourself within the satire of this collection, neither should you. This isn't about me. This isn't about you. This is a play. We're all players. Remember ... know your role? Play your part? This is about the disillusionment of them and our consciousness surrounding our performances based on the preconceptions and (non)adherence to whiteness. It was imperative for me to experiment with holding their gaze hostage. My hope is that others in the pursuit of experimentation, freedom, and truth will pick up this book and be inspired to do the same.

Thank you to Elaine Katzenberger, Garrett Caples, and all the folks at City Lights for believing in this project. Thank you to Toya Groves for being my backbone in the Bay. Thank you to my sisters, Sheila, Leila and Meca, who were patrons to me while I finished this book. Sheila! You made it. Your name is in print, girl! Thank you to my parents who value my artistic antics. I am the loved, respected & undisputed drama queen of my family. Thank you to William Johnson Jr., my momager and best friend. A forever thank you to Truong Tran, who somehow manages to see me through my crazy literary interrogations. And thank you to the readers for picking up this book and holding its universe. I hope you walked away feeling dizzy. As always, I'd like to thank myself. From the last collection to this one, I'm a cycle closer to my highest form, and I will continue to bet on myself. Until next time . . .